D0919483

Ex Libris

DISCARD

DISCARD

New CLASSIC INTERIORS

New CLASSIC INTERIORS

ALESSANDRA BRANCA

Written with Christine Pittel

Principal Photography by Thibault Jeanson

Design by Doug Turshen with David Huang

Stewart, Tabori & Chang, New York

DEDICATION

To my Steve...
whose unconditional love, unlimited patience, great wisdom,
and tremendous support I could not live without.

R0425179682

CONTENTS

**I** never set out to do a book on my work—I was asked many times but didn't feel my work was "there" yet. I then realized it will never be "there" as it is a work in progress. This book represents a series of informally collected concepts that are the basis of my design "philosophy". It is a very small representation of over twenty-five years of work. Many hours, months, and sometimes years went into the making of these seemingly effortless looks. There have been amazing bonds forged in this process with clients, architects, trades, and staff—each as important as the other.

My work has been blessed with much celebration by press and clients alike—all this is too humbling for words. I deeply believe you only get what you put into something and this body of material shows the joy, warmth, pleasure, and spirit that went into it. When you take into account the tremendous discipline this field requires, the amount of work each detail takes, the supportive clients, the incredible associations with great craftsmen, and the support of tremendously dedicated staff, you would think it would be enough to make for incredible work; but the truth is in the end it is a little bit of magic and exuberance that makes it special. Like a great meal, the success is in the planning, ingredients, skills, and, last but not least, the spark of spontaneity that makes it sing.

Branca is about detail, color, culture, and comfort. Whether I work on a city apartment, a beach house, a country property or a loft, the principles are the same. Everything needs a proper plan to start. Each space is created to accommodate the needs and personality of that specific client and project. Similar to creating a business plan, I set out with very specific goals, accounting for where my clients are in their lives and where they are going. Challenges are identified, issues addressed, scope defined, and then begins the fun stuff.

Can't you imagine some Roman centurion in that helmet? It stands in front of one of our family bulletin boards. A bulletin board has always struck me as a way to turn your life into your art. Snapshots, invitations, and images that catch my eye get tacked up into an impromptu collage. Every so often I take everything off and start all over again.

The process is essential, but then you need that spark—the collection of images, experiences, and dreams that make a project what it is. I encourage everyone to do as so many have said before me—collect images of things you love, that inspire you and make you happy. All that matters in the end—once the furniture is laid out, the window treatments are hung, and the art is collected—is that you never want to leave that place; that your home makes you sublimely happy. The process is a complicated one and the road can be quite arduous, but the results are always worth the effort.

I never imagined I'd be a decorator when I grew up—a lawyer, architect, fashion designer or princess, but not a decorator. While I prepared for a career in law, little did I know I'd use that topic in my business. When I studied Rome's architecture in awe, little did I know it would be the inspiration for so many designs in my work. When I obsessed about fashion, little did I know that knowledge of textiles and workmanship would find its way into draperies and interiors. When I dreamt about life as a princess, little did I know I'd be happier making others live like royalty in their own homes. We are all where we are meant to be.

Living is the operative word. When I design a home, there are always plenty of places where you can curl up with a book and a glass of wine. I try to anticipate every need—a lamp next to the chair where you're likely to sit; a table within arm's reach for that glass. It is perfectly possible for a room to be beautiful yet practical. For me, it's not enough that a room look good. It also has to work. I put an incredible amount of effort into making people feel comfortable. It's part of my nature. I can't imagine a space without those who will inhabit it. Their passions and interests give a home character. Designing is about much more than bricks, mortar, sofas and window treatments. I try to give a little Italian soul to a house and those living in it.

So sit back, relax, and enjoy a glimpse of a few of my favorite interiors.

The inlaid stone on the floor and the rusticated walls, painted to look like stone, set up a lot of strong geometries in this entrance hall. So I kept the furnishings simple and equally strong. The Regency settee, upholstered in a wonderful paprika red, and the unusual table throw in a few curves. Even the lanterns have interesting, austere lines.

Warmth, **Abund**

Exuberance, Inger

Luxury, *Softnes*

Symmetry, *Prop*

Texture, **Personali**

Practicality, Deli

Ease, **Quality,** *P*

Organized, Han

Unexpected, **Vib**

Sensual, *Lush,* U

Exotic, **Stron**

ance, *Intimacy,*
nuity, **Originality,**
, Comfort, *Scale,*
ortion, **Balance,**
ty, Glamour, Energy,
cacy, **Charm,** *Wit,*
Playful, Efficient,
dsome, **Dreamy**
rant, *Spirited,*
plifting **Inspiring,**
, *Enchanting.*

I. ROME

In Rome, if you're bored, walk outside and your life changes.

The architectural details on this sixteenth-century palazzo are so classical and clean—Pompeian red and an ocher so rich and mellow it almost glows. These are the colors I think of when I think of Rome.

Why Rome? Because it is where everything started for me. I find it very reassuring to shop for my family's meals at the open-air market in the Campo dei Fiori, the same market that has been there since the sixteenth century. The fruit vendor's stall is a picture of *abbondanza*—glorious abundance—with apricots and peaches and grapes arranged in perfect heaps. Even the pharmacist around the corner has somehow managed to make the medications in his window look utterly appealing! To be born in Rome is to be born with the design gene. Italians have an instinct for beauty, and my eye was honed by my upbringing. My grandfather was an art historian and critic for the Vatican City newspaper, and one of my earliest memories is of trying to get my nose over a display case at the Vatican Museum. I was so small that he had to lift me up to see the exhibits inside. He would pose my hands—with the little finger just so—to mimic a figure in a painting by Guercino.

Around every corner in Rome there is another majestic building. You may be standing in line at the bank, but don't forget to look up at the ceiling or you'll miss a magnificent fresco. The great masterworks of art and architecture become as familiar as old friends. My concept of color was formed by Raphael and Giotto; my sense of scale and proportion was shaped by Bramante and Borromini. After school, I would duck into a favorite church on my way home, thrilled to know I was walking on the same cobblestones as Michelangelo. Those basalt cobblestones are like a river that flows through the city, taking you from one neighborhood to another, and one century to another.

This is the newsstand right behind our house where I buy the newspaper every morning. Afterward, we might sit in the piazza and have a coffee and read the paper. The street is painted with the symbol of the local soccer team. And what are the colors? Red and yellow!

And one café to another. The city is ancient and gregarious. In Rome, you don't spend your life inside, confined by four walls. You live outdoors, at café and restaurant tables that spill onto the street. I might start my day with a coffee and cornetto—an Italian croissant—at the corner bar. Then a quick run to the market, where I let the catch of the day and the vegetables of the season determine what we are going to eat: artichokes in the fall, the first tender stalks of asparagus in spring. I have to visit the mushroom vendor and the cheese man. Of course I cannot come home without flowers, and I stop to talk to Adele, who has been selling flowers to me for thirty years. We Italians do not buy mixed bouquets. We buy a big mass of something, like lilies or roses or cornflowers. If the family is home for lunch, I'll cook. If we go out for lunch, it will usually be to an old standby, like Il Bolognese or Nino's, where I've been going my whole life! Dinner might be at Pierluigi around the corner under the stars. Then I may go out to visit a museum. On the way, I might stop by one of my own personal stations of the Cross, Santa Maria sopra Minerva—the only Gothic church in Rome, built directly on the foundations of Pompey's temple to Minerva. The vault of the nave is painted a vivid cerulean blue and dotted with stars. Outside in the square is one of those sculptures that always make me smile—Bernini's whimsical white marble baby elephant, balancing an Egyptian obelisk on his back.

Walk over to the next square, and you'll find my favorite structure in Rome, which I pass every single day—the Pantheon. Dating back to AD 125, it is the most ancient building in Rome to survive relatively intact. Every time I look at all the layers of marble and mosaics and paint, I see something different. Animals were once sacrificed and burned under the huge dome, and the smoke would escape through the oculus, which is still open to the sky. On a brilliant day, the light that pours down is celestial, but on a rainy day the play of light is breathtaking.

When I am done with wandering, I may stop at a café and sit outside under an umbrella to read the newspaper. Even late at night, you will still see people sitting out in the piazza, finishing up discussions after dinner. What other people think of as the cacophony of Rome—motor scooters, horns, and the conversations that never end—is as soothing to me as the hum of bees. I would feel that something was amiss without it.

Even though I have lived in Chicago for thirty or so years, I still feel as if I am coming home when we arrive in Rome. My children tease me: "How can you think of yourself as Italian after so many years in the States?" But I do. I always will. Rome feeds my soul. I want my children to understand their roots, and to know my Rome, which is why my husband, Steve, and I decided it made sense to find an apartment of our own here. I purposely looked only in a very old neighborhood, and I focused on one particular street, the Via Giulia. It was created by Pope Julius II in the sixteenth century to link various government institutions and lead pilgrims to the Vatican, so it's wider than the norm. That means the buildings on either side get more light, which was the big attraction for me. Our building used to house the priests from a rectory, but it was bombed during World War II and very little of the original interior detailing was left. In one way, that is an advantage (I like to think positively). It means we don't have to worry about six-hundred-year-old plumbing or set out strategically placed pots when it rains. The kitchen, bathroom, and electrical wiring are new, which is terribly convenient!

The front door opens into a large entryway. I didn't want to waste the space, so I furnished it with comfortable chairs and a big table to double as a study. Since it gets great light, it's also the place where my mother does her drawing and painting. It is nice to walk into a space and immediately plunge into the thick of things. The window treatments are plain linen, just pulled back and draped over classic iron hooks. It gets very hot in the summer in Rome, and you don't want layers and layers of fabric.

In the living room, everything is practical and relaxed. This is where we really live—where we read, work, talk. In Italy, there is no such thing as a family room. Why would you need such a room? It already exists as the living room *is* the family room. Children are not relegated off to some space of their own, but enfolded into the midst of any gathering. Most entertaining is done at home, and the space has to be able to expand and contract so you can accommodate more people. That's why you will always see lots of chairs and stools in an Italian home. At a moment's notice, you might want to fit a few more people around the table. Our living room doubles as a dining room, which is why I was particularly happy

to find that Renaissance Revival desk. The top opens up and leaves pull out from each side, and I can seat twelve people!

The idea is to create rooms that can multitask. My husband can be working at the desk in the living room while my mother is painting in the entryway and my children can be watching a soccer game. In an old house like this, the rooms open right into each other, which encourages interaction. You don't even have to be in the same room, yet you still feel part of it all. After my morning marketing, I have the latest neighborhood gossip from the butcher. Meanwhile my mother has been to the framer's shop and knows all about the people who have just moved in next door. The children come home and are full of stories about the places they have been and the friends they have met. It's just not possible for them to walk in and vanish into their rooms. Of course it helps that in Italian apartments, the public spaces are large, but the bedrooms are small. Italians don't spend a lot of time in the bedroom during the day. We use a bedroom only to sleep.

As a result, this is a place where the focus is on being together as a family. One son may be helping me in the kitchen while the other keeps one eye on his laptop as my daughter regales us with tales of her afternoon's adventures. My husband has set aside his book. For a rare moment, my mother is doing absolutely nothing. There is a sense of togetherness and ease and comfort. In Rome, I have found a way to bring us all home.

I love details. I'm

In the entryway, the original ceiling beams are exposed and offer a dark contrast to the ocher plaster walls, which become a more mellow yellow in the afternoon sun. Stag horns flank an eighteenth-century Dutch tortoiseshell mirror, hung over a nineteenth-century painted Northern Italian table. OPPOSITE: Our own little foot fetish. These plaster molds, tucked under the table, are taken from various classical statues. We have one for each member of the family, set on old Roman bricks collected by my mother. They add a touch of fantasy as soon as you walk in. A very subtle family portrait!

obsessed with them.

I don't do period rooms, although I may follow or be inspired by classical principles.

Symmetry, proportion, and practicality determined the placement of the furniture in the entryway. The delicately carved eighteenth-century Italian chair—covered in the original old cracked leather the color of dark toffee—has beautiful lines. The bookcase is actually an armoire (those books are faux) and provides additional storage. The Louis Philippe reclining bergere offers another great moment to sit and relax.

SPICE

Exotic fabrics like ikats and suzanis and paisleys add a little spice to a room. I love the fact that this is a Roman living room, but the fabrics come from farflung areas like India, Turkey, and Uzbekistan. Weaving paisley through the room is an interesting detail; here used as a throw, to drape a table, and to upholster two chairs. I realize it's unusual to put paisley on a French bergère, but it relaxes it and makes it less formal. Paisley is one of those textiles that creates instant warmth. If you keep your eyes open at flea markets for paisley shawls, you can often find them in good condition. If the weave is sturdy enough, they can easily be used to upholster a chair. If it is not, consider making a lampshade with them!

A mix of fabrics adds life to the living room. The sofas are upholstered in chenille, the ottoman is covered in a 1960s woven stripe, and the lampshade is made out of an old sari. The unusual eighteenth-century giltwood sconce is shaped like an urn and echoes the shield in the painted panel above the sofa. I saw that panel in an antiques shop and fell in love with it. Paul Brill, a Flemish artist who worked in Rome during the seventeenth century, painted it; it portrays a cardinal's family crest. The hand bearing flowers is the symbol of friendship. On Christmas morning, during our first Christmas in this apartment, I opened a card from my husband and there was a picture of that hand holding flowers. That's how I knew he had gone back to the shop and bought the panel for me. In this photograph, you get to see it twice: It's reflected in the mirror on the right, above the other sofa.

I think a room should be open to all sorts of possibilities.

When we're ready to eat, we just pull out the concealed leaves of the desk to expand it into a dining table. The chairs can be folded up and set aside when they're not needed. The windows—and the light they let in—are beautiful, and I saw no reason to cover them up with elaborate window treatments. The curtains are hung from simple iron poles. For the fabric, I made my own stripe, picking up the paisley from the other side of the room and alternating it with plain linen. Vertical stripes make a room feel even taller. The armoire on the left is made of steel and was built in the nineteenth century to safeguard documents. I softened it with ticking inside, and use it to store all our liqueurs, glassware, and table linens. The fax and the printer live in that Chinese sideboard on the right—you wouldn't know it, but our living room also functions as an office.

I bought the tulips and all the food on the table at the market in the morning. OPPOSITE: In this small corner off the kitchen, I decided to go for it and make it feel even more intimate by painting the walls a dark plum. We eat breakfast here and sometimes lunch. Above the bench, I hung four still lifes by my mother, Anna Chiara Branca. They are painted to look as if they were frescoes, complete with a few stray butterflies and insects.

THE BED

I grew up in a culture where bedrooms are not sitting rooms where you entertain other people. A bedroom is where you have your most intimate and quiet time. The bed is the focal point of the room, and you might choose something that is a pleasure to look at and very comfortable as well. This distinctive iron bed is a modern version of a *lit à la Polonaise*. Historically, the framework would have been swathed in fabric, creating an elaborate canopy and bed curtains to keep out the drafts. But with central heating, that's no longer necessary and frankly, I love the way it looks all on its own. It is so sculptural; the steel is like a line drawing in space. It's a great way to bring a little detail to the architecture in a room that lacks it. The bed is the first thing you see. Find an interesting one, and it can make the room.

The walls in my bedroom are a pale mossy green, and the window treatments are made of a silk green-and-beige ticking. A Louis XVI painted settee at the foot of the bed doesn't take up much room and gives you another place to sit down. The Pompeian-inspired frescoes in trompe l'oeil faux stone frames, done by my mother, make the room feel very peaceful.

I have no fear of color.

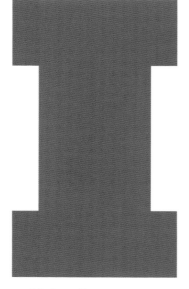

I grew up in a culture that is saturated with color. You can't help but love it. It bombards you. Think of the scarlet reds and cobalt blues of Italian Renaissance paintings. The architecture of Italy—yellow stucco walls dripping with ivy, terra-cotta tiles—is suffused with color. Italian fashion pulses with color. And Italian food—as simple as a dish of tomatoes and mozzarella and basil—is a bright flag of red, white, and green. Even the earth of Italy is not brown; it's red, as if it has been baked in the sun for centuries.

That Italian love of color, embodied in the deep rich reds and the golden ochers of Rome, has seeped into my work. Color is so much a part of my being that I wouldn't know how to exist without it. I cannot think of form without color. Color can expand a space or turn a small room into a jewel box. Color is my accent, my punctuation. For me, there is no emotion without color.

Color is comfortable. It gives warmth to a room. I always start with the shell first, and I try to solve any problems that stem from the architecture. I consider the way the space will be used and plan what furniture it will need. Then we think of the styling of the furniture and finally only then do I begin thinking about color and pattern and how I will layer it in. It's a very painterly process, and I've learned a lot about color from studying art. Raphael has taught me intensity. Titian has trained me in nuance. Tiepolo, with his celestial blues, has coached me in clarity, and Caravaggio has instructed me in the mysteries of dark and light.

This is a second home in Florida for a wonderful couple. Their *joie de vivre* was contagious, and it shows in their house. When you don't live in a space year-round, it's easier to be more adventuresome. We had fun with the iconic Palm Beach pink and green, and I added a touch of chinoiserie. Who wouldn't smile at the sight of that pagoda lantern (also in pink and green) with bells tinkling in the breeze? Most people would look at this dining table (actually an old table that we ebonized) and think it should be white, just like the chairs. No, no, no. A touch of black here and there exalts the rest of the colors.

The way we perceive color has everything to do with the quality of light. A yellow that looks great in Santa Fe may seem too bright in Chicago. Color has a symbiotic relationship with place, and certain places are associated with certain colors. I feel it is very important to take this into account. Venice has that shimmering light, reflected off the canals, and Venetians use a lot of watery blues and greens. Nothing could be brighter than the colors of India, where the oranges and pinks are spectacular. Historically, Venice was the gateway to the exotic East and borrowed its brilliant jewel tones. Farther north in Sweden, you see those soothing gray-blues. This is where I realized that color doesn't have to be strong to be expressive. When I think of St. Petersburg, I remember lemon yellows and baby blues. Belgium and the Netherlands are more sober, with a muted palette of taupe and cream and gray, set off by those graphic black-and-white marble floors.

Color is a celebration of life. Why is it that places that are all white, like Antarctica, are usually devoid of people? If you don't feel comfortable with color on the walls, you can bring in a shot of color with accessories, like pillows and porcelain, or a piece of painted furniture. A red-lacquered Chinese cabinet can have a galvanizing effect on a room. If clients don't know what colors they like, I'll often try to draw it out of them by looking at the clothes they wear and asking where they like to travel. Color is such an expression of personality. Even the humblest house in Rome has a pot of red geraniums on the windowsill.

This space is one of my very favorites. We turned a sun porch at the beach into a tented fantasy, hung with miles of white linen trimmed in moss-green grosgrain ribbon. It's like a luxurious beach cabana, and when the window treatments are closed, it becomes a cozy guest room. The daybed is one of a pair. If you pull on the cast-iron starfish at the bottom, it opens into a trundle bed. Linens are stored in the columns on each side. Children love the ottoman, which is shaped like a donut and covered in Naugahyde so it can be used indoors or out. With a tile floor, maintenance is simple: Just sweep away the sand and relax.

ESTRO

There's a word in Italian, *estro*, which means "spark." It's the driving force, that little zing that makes a person or a thing original and unique. This room has *estro*. It starts with the big one-foot-wide stripe on the walls. It's in two tones, to give it more depth. Then there's that traditional toile in a very unconventional palette—lime green and hot pink. The striped cushions on the rattan chairs pick up the colors, and the ottoman is covered in a pink leopard print. This is clearly not your grandmother's Palm Beach! We didn't take the room too seriously, which is part of its charm. I remember buying some of the furniture at the shops along the Dixie Highway, before it was chic to shop there.

The dining table is part of the living room, but if you want to make it more private you could move the screen in between. A nineteenth-century bamboo cabinet holds seashells and dishes. The rug is sisal, which adds great texture and is very durable. I slipcovered the furniture for practicality. That pink-and-green stripe on the rattan chair is actually an outdoor fabric. You can come in wearing a wet bathing suit and sit anywhere.

Most people find red exciting. I think it's calming.

To make a large bedroom feel more intimate, I covered the walls in a red cashmere-and-wool felt. It's as if you wrapped a great big blanket around the room. It would be hard to get this depth and intensity of color with paint—it would take too much pigment. In order to achieve a certain effect, you first have to figure out which material to use, because the same shade of red will look very different depending on the material. Fabric reacts differently to light than paint. This felt absorbs light, rather than reflecting it, which makes the red darker. I had it backed with paper and glued onto the wall, instead of upholstering it, so it's flat rather than cushy. That gives the room a crisp quality, which is enhanced by the tailored white bed linens, outlined in black.

A cashmere throw tossed over a chair adds a little softness. The window treatments are made of wool sateen and trimmed with a custom-made Greek key trim that picks up the red and the black. OPPOSITE: I like the contrast of the shiny black-lacquered Louis XV bureau plot against the matte red felt on the walls. Touches of ormulu add a nice gleam. The brass bouillotte lamp is an eighteenth-century classic, named after a French card game similar to poker. (Its dish-shaped base would have held the chips.) As the candles burned, the tole shade (which wouldn't burn) could be lowered with a turn of the screw-key to keep the light out of the players' eyes. It's one of my favorite types of lamp.

I wanted this Chicago duplex to feel like an Italian palazzo.

The apartment faces Lake Michigan, and the light off the water in winter can be cold and gray, so I countered that with warm Italian yellows and ochers. The plaster walls are striated and glazed in several different shades of yellow, to make them look ancient. It's a big, cozy room, with a fireplace to the side of those two sofas and a piano near the door. The doors are actually seventeenth-century-style, with a diamond pattern that inspired the faux-painted ceiling. We added a few beams to create a more dynamic effect. The room displays a mix of contemporary art—with beautiful English and Chinese antiques. The sofa is upholstered in a yellow angora mohair, and the club chairs are covered in a tree-of-life pattern, with red squiggles on a yellow ground that ends up softening the overall effect of the pattern. That's why I always say you have to walk away and look at a fabric sample from a distance, before you decide. You should like it from far away as well as close-up.

When I'm choosing fabrics for a room, I look for a good balance. That balance is achieved by taking all the parts and putting them together and then filling in with those that will make the space sing. OPPOSITE: Chinese lacquer work, as far as I'm concerned, is an art form. The rule of thumb was seventeen coats of lacquer, sanded in between, and each layer of color is never exactly the same. The final effect is the culmination of all those shades. There's something very Zen about that to me. This eighteenth-century cabinet was retrofitted as a bar which makes it that much more important—furniture as art *and* function.

I love chinoiserie.

Scale—is that object too big or too small for the space? It's a question that a designer answers almost instinctively. There are no rules. I'm always playing with scale, juxtaposing large and small furnishings to create intriguing compositions. Large-scale objects in a small room may seem counterintuitive, but they can make a small space feel larger. It's a delicate balance.

This penthouse apartment, built in the 1920s, with twenty-two-foot ceilings and Gothic Revival stone windows, embodies the power of scale. What type of window treatments could possibly live up to windows like that? We did drop-dead balloon shades (which were originally designed in eighteenth-century England) in a custom-made golden yellow damask with a ten-inch fringe—motorized to go up or down at the push of a button. I designed a custom Turkish-style sofa and slipper chairs and covered them in a striped velvet. A vintage zebra rug adds more graphic pattern, strong enough to stand up to the space.

I love tradition, but I won't let it confine me.

The extraordinary seventeenth-century linenfold paneling in this living room could have been very serious, but we played against that with the St. Hubert carved deer heads, a purchase of the clients at auction, on either side of the fireplace. We restored the oak, but decided not to clean decades of burn marks off the mantel because we liked the sense of age. All the colors in the room were taken from that gigantic heraldic flag, which the client bought at the Duke of Windsor sale. It's the royal standard of the House of Windsor, which King Edward VIII took with him when he abdicated. The red-and-gold damask on the Georgian-style slipper chair has movement and scale. So does the nineteenth-century English needlepoint rug, which almost seems to imitate the Gothic Revival fretwork on the plaster ceiling. The large oval ottoman is upholstered in leopard-patterned silk velvet with a fourteen-inch custom bullion fringe. Bullion fringe looks fanciful, but its origins are practical. People used it at the bottoms of furniture in place of fabric, which would often get stained with shoe polish.

Great scale can be exhilarating.

With its soaring ceilings and hand-carved paneling, this is a magnificent room. In a huge space like this, the challenge is to create intimacy. I broke it up into several seating areas and added a big round skirted table as a focal point. You could pull one of the chairs over and look at a book, or set the table with platters of hors d'oeuvres when you're having a party. The three main areas in the room are separate but interrelated by the repetition of yellow and red and gold. Color can hold a large space together and generate warmth. If you look at the whole room as a painting, you'll notice that there's a balance of light and dark colors, solid and patterned fabrics. Together, they blend into an ensemble and create a rich complexity. Thank you Caravaggio for the inspiration!

A SHOT OF RED

Red is exuberant. Red makes me happy. Some scientists think that it's the first color we "see" in the womb. Historically, there's Chinese red, Pompeian red, American-flag red. So many cultures have embraced it, and they can't all be wrong! I've rarely done a home without a touch of red. It sparks up a room and gives it life. But if you're wary about color, you don't have to do the whole room in red. You could pick out just one element, like the lampshades or the pillows, and do those. In this room, the lampshades are like bright exclamation points amid all the neutrals. It's a small thing, but repeating it over and over again creates a big impact. Then, if you get tired of red, you can easily change them to another color, which would make it feel like a whole new room.

Believe it or not, this was originally an office building. The apartment, (redeveloped CS residential space when I first saw it) was a stark concrete box. We added the crown moldings, floors, and the antique columns to give it some detail. The furniture—a Louis XVI settee, a William IV mahogany center table—contribute to the classical feeling. I designed the mahogany and gilt bookcases, the slipper chairs, and the stools around the table. The stools are covered in my signature overscaled stripe, made from two fabrics—in this case, red silk and off-white velvet. Red is like a trail of Hansel and Gretel's bread crumbs, leading you through the room. It adds another layer of sophistication and spirit.

Every room needs a touch of black to give it depth.

OPPOSITE: Black frames, black curtain rods, and a black-lacquered secretary stand out against the Naples yellow walls in this sitting room. Black keeps the yellow from getting too sweet, and the yellow keeps the black from feeling too harsh. The combination actually makes both colors look stronger. In an effort to add even more interest and depth, I had the walls stenciled a damask pattern. Naples yellow is such a beautiful shade for a room that faces west, because it radiates warmth in the light of the setting sun. I upped the heat quotient with red striated velvet on the painted Louis XVI footstool and red cashmere throws tossed over the chairs. Early on in my career, I realized that wherever there's a window, at night there's a black hole. So I'll always make an effort to put a lamp close by, often with a red lampshade. Friends tell me that when they walk down the street at night, they can always identify a house I've done from the windows. They glow. RIGHT: The daybed opens up into a trundle bed. I would rather have a sitting room that doubles as a guest room than a room that only works as a guest room and is rarely used. My mother, a renowned botanical artist, did the watercolors of tulips.

You can get away with hot pink. You just have to be judicious.

This sitting room/office belongs to the lady of the house and started with that great toile in an unusual color combination—hot pink and brown—that puts a new twist on a classic. Since there wasn't all that much wall, I decided to paint it hot pink as well. I have learned over the years that you can have too much of a good thing, but here it doesn't feel overwhelming because the room is so open. I picked up the pink on the leather ottoman and trimmed it in brown, and conversely the brown sofa is outlined with a pink contrast welt. The big round mirror over the fireplace is a play on the big round windows in the family room on the floor below, just beyond the railings.

A wall isn't just a wall. It's an opportunity. If you have a small room, don't be afraid to paint it a dark color. It makes it far more dramatic and interesting. I lacquered this small hall outside the master bedroom in a deep, dark brown the color of semisweet chocolate. The 1940s console is painted white, with a mirrored top. Against the darkness, you really appreciate the shape. I like to think of furniture as sculpture.

The mirrored top on the 1940s console, and the fact that you can practically see yourself in the lacquer, meant I really didn't need more mirror, so I hung a wonderful drawing over the console. The silver frame and the silver candlesticks add their own sparkle, reflected in the mirrored panels on the French doors. White plaster neo-Baroque sconces have that fanciful 1940s look. The floor is ebonized, which makes the white baseboards stand out even more.

Color is like music. Amid brown and white, you hear a note of blue. The browns and the whites create a lovely play of dark and light, but it's the unexpected hit of turquoise that energizes the room. The walls are done in Venetian plaster, except for the window bay, which is upholstered in the same Fortuny fabric as the window treatments. The Louis XVI–style painted bergères are Jansen, covered in a chocolate brown silk velvet, a color that reappears on the headboard's trim and the lampshades on the Emile-Jacques Ruhlmann desk. The floors are bare, except for the zebra rug and the linen mats (called *scendiletto*) on either side of the bed. That's very Italian. They needed them on their cold marble floors, and it's nice to have the first thing your feet touch in the morning be fresh and clean. When I was growing up, mine were embroidered with *buon giorno* and *buona notte!*

The Venini glass table, made in the 1970s,
strikes a brilliant blue note that echoes
throughout the room. OPPOSITE: Oxblood
red against deep turquoise blue—it's the
unusual juxtaposition of colors that makes
this vignette so intriguing. The vases stand
on a desk and add a vibrant accent to a
predominantly neutral room.

ABOVE: The beautiful 1940s Venetian mirror above the mantel is inset with blue glass, and that gave me the idea to use blue as an accent throughout this bedroom. The butterflies are simply the most vivid version of this hue—Mother Nature at her best! OPPOSITE: The Venetian plaster walls in this bath are a watery blue-green, and it took ten tries to get it exactly right. I picked up the same color for the shade. That extraordinary tub, in iron and porcelain, came from London and weighs hundreds of pounds. We had to reinforce the floor for it! A tub is often the elephant in the room, but this one reflects the light, which makes it seem almost immaterial.

Your bedroom should be a refuge from the rest of the world.

Imagine how it would feel to be enveloped in this ethereal blue. I used the same pale washed silk everywhere—on the walls, on the curtains, and on the canopy bed, which is like a room within a room. It's luxurious and private—and also offers a great place to play hide-and-seek. The crenellated detail is something you might see on an early eighteenth-century pelmet, but I've taken it a lot less seriously. I smile every time I see those dangling tassels—they're completely whimsical and very chic. The blue is one of those indescribable colors, inspired by the color of the client's eyes. Sometimes it's more blue and sometimes it's more gray. It shifts as the light changes over the course of a day.

I have so much fun with the details. I'm completely compulsive, which is probably why I do this for a living. Think of all the work that went into threading those vintage beads onto this tassel. It's like a piece of jewelry for the room. OPPOSITE. CLOCKWISE FROM TOP LEFT: We had miles of this looped trim, and the jaunty tassels, made in exactly the same shade as the silk. Feathers are an unexpected touch on a silk pillow, next to a curtain embroidered with flowers. White silk is gathered around a pale blue silk rosette on this Napoleonic gilt-bronze light fixture. A Greek key trim accents the classical lines of a black and gilt Regency chaise.

Seven-foot-tall engravings of a fork and a spoon. Why not?

OPPOSITE: **It's a very playful thing to do in a kitchen, and certainly makes it memorable. I always try to find room for an eat-in area. The clients can pull up a stool and have informal wine tastings at the island; their wine cellar is behind the glass door. You can see I love stripes. I even did them on the floor, with alternating bands of light and dark walnut.** RIGHT: **Metal-and-glass shelves by the stove are set in front of a mirror, which seems to expand the space. The hanging lights, made of gleaming nickel, have that chic industrial look.**

COLOR COMBINATIONS

Apple green and orange, turquoise and chocolate brown, plum and taupe—these are just a few of my favorite unusual combinations. I'm always studying how colors look together and trying to find new relationships. Sometimes I might use one color alone, but usually I think in terms of a palette. You have to treat color in context. Put your choices all together and see how they look in the room where they're going to be. The light in each room—and each region of a country—is unique and will affect the way they read. I like to do a thirty-six-inch-square paint sample on cardboard, and then fold it to see how the color reflects upon itself. Colors reverberate, which is one reason they look darker on the walls. Every painter will also tell you that you need a proper base coat in order to get depth and intensity. You have to be a bit of a chemist, but it's worth it when you get it just right.

During the Empire period, when Napoleon was emperor of France, people experimented with daring color combinations like purple and acid green, usually in stripes or solid fabrics—florals didn't take over until the late nineteenth century. This guest room is an exuberant rush of orange and green. When the colors are wild, you want the shapes to be very clean. The tester is hung on rods—very straightforward—with a crisp crenellated edge. The pillow on the bed is a simple bolster. That swath of orange looks particularly bold against a green wall. How do you know if you've gone too far? Decorating is like cooking. If you're adding some spice, you have to stir in a little bit at a time and taste it as you go. And as you get better with practice, at some point you leave the recipe behind and start to improvise. It's just a matter of what works for your taste buds and your eye.

I like to layer and juxtapose patterns to create energy.

I see pattern everywhere. The wood on the old hayloft doors in our coach house forms a chevron pattern, which I accentuated with black and white paint. It turned the doors into a great piece of modern art. The white slipcovered chair and the black velvet-trimmed pillow hold on the powerful graphics.

When I was in India, everywhere I went I saw men wearing paisley shawls. The shawl would be wrapped around their head and shoulders in the morning. Then, as the day wore on and it got progressively hotter, it would move to their shoulders, and then their hips, until finally they would take it off entirely and sit on it. This soft, colorful cloth is always with them. It almost seems to live and breathe. Traditionally, the finest paisley cloth was woven by men, but the origins of the teardrop-shaped *boteh* motif have been obscured over time. Is it a flower, a tadpole, a cypress tree, or a seed? Whatever the facts, the pattern clearly has power. It has become a symbol of life and eternity and one of my most favorite!

Italian damask, French toile, English chintz—in each pattern, you can trace a whole world. Every culture develops its own characteristic patterns, embedded with centuries of history and tradition. Pattern holds memories. It can quickly take us back to a particular place and time. A soft, faded floral has connotations of wonderful old country cottages and a quieter, gentler era. It conveys emotion. I rarely do a room without pattern. It adds color and texture and movement. Pattern is a part of life.

Some of the most beautiful patterns come from nature. Think of intertwining vines and leaves, or flowers and branches. I love those blowsy English roses printed on linen that almost looks as if it has been tea-dyed. Then there are the glorious French printed cottons,

I upholstered the walls with toile to turn a small bedroom into a cozy cocoon. Then I outlined the room, and the window, with black grosgrain ribbon. Otherwise the window would have disappeared. I love how modern the black lines made it feel—the striped bed picks up the same colors but adds a strong contrast to balance the sweetness of the toile.

Every-one can put their feet up in this room.

It's on the second floor of our coach house, which used to be the hayloft but now is where my children watch TV or hang out with their friends. Oh, if these walls could talk! The room is done in red and black and cream—a palette that always works for me—and there's a nice mix of patterns and solids, old and new, light and dark. There's a durable ticking on the sofas. The paisleys add another layer of color and pattern, and the big red leather ottoman gives the room its zing. The Dutch-style mirror is new; the pediment, which purportedly came from a Robert Adam house, is old. I bought it at auction; it dates back to the eighteenth century.

still being made today in tree-of-life patterns that date back to the eighteenth century. You can see earlier versions in the grand old chateaux in the Loire Valley. In Rome, I grew up with the subtle intricacies of Italian damask—all tone-on-tone and matte versus sheen, so the pattern catches and plays with the light.

But my absolute favorite, the one pattern I can't live without, is stripes. I love how clean they look. There's a crispness to the geometry, and you can get such interesting color combinations. It's a very particular look—the colors touch but don't mix. If you think of decorating like cooking, a straightforward black-and-white stripe is like salt—it brings out the flavor of the other ingredients. An exotic paisley is more like cardamom—it adds a little spice.

I like to play one pattern off another. My kind of decorating is all about layering, and I have no qualms about mixing high and low. In the same room, you will see luxurious damask next to humble ticking. That feels very fresh and modern to me. It's like wearing an elegant silk shirt and jeans. I paint with pattern. I will use it on the walls, on the furniture, and on the floor. Pattern is a way to give depth to a space. Like an artist, I'm using color and texture and pattern and form to create a composition. When I'm choosing fabric for a room, I'll often vary the scale so I end up with a small-, medium-, and large-scale pattern, which creates a certain sense of balance. But that's just a guideline, not a hard-and-fast rule.

Pattern is forgiving. If a client has a favorite chair where I know they are going to sit all the time, I will cover it in a pattern. Pattern wears well. It will show less wear than a solid, neutral fabric. It is practical and elegant at the same time.

On the other side of the old hayloft is a desk and a bookcase, both of which I had made. They're done in black, with dramatic touches of red. The desk is topped with red tooled leather, and so are the pull-out shelves on the bookcase. I always build those into a piece like this, so you can reach for a book and set it right down and look through it easily. The inside of the bookcase is also painted red. That shakes it up a bit, but I admit it's a little hard to see now that the shelves are so jammed with books! The simple linen Roman shades are trimmed with wooden tassels, just for fun.

ABOVE: The architectural elements of this staircase create a pattern of dark and light, which is echoed in the collection of black-and-white photographs and continued in the honeycomb pattern of the wonderful David Hicks carpet (OPPOSITE). It's relatively safe to indulge a passion for pattern in a space you merely pass through, like this. A patterned carpet is also practical, and it certainly makes the hallway less boring. Suddenly walking up and down all those stairs is more fun!

Pattern is not limited to the fabric on a chair. It can be architectural as well. Here, in this entryway, it starts with the rusticated stone on the walls, which is actually made out of medium-density fiberboard, cut, laid, and painted to look like stone. Good architecture will give any room a head start, and if it isn't there to begin with, you can create it. It's important to get the shell of a room right, first.

}

A skirted table softens the stone. It's also a great solution while you're still searching for that incredible console. You could have sawhorses and plywood under there—and storage boxes—and no one would know! The chocolate brown felt is trimmed with a Greek key appliqué and topped with glass. That wavy red velvet in the fabric on the Georgian chairs adds a nice twist to all the right angles.

BALANCE

I chose to work with a lot of pattern in
this room, but it works because it's all in
the same basic colors of red, green, and
beige. That rustic, handblocked linen in an
eighteenth-century tree-of-life pattern is one
of my favorites. I had it quilted for the sofa,
which is something I often do. The cotton
batting makes it very soft, and the fabric
seems to wear even better because it's not
pulled tight, as in conventional upholstery.
That green velvet-and-cotton stripe has the
three-dimensional quality I love. I used it
in concentric squares on the pillows and
to line the curtain swags, which makes
them even more graphic. Red strie velvet
on the ottoman gives the room a bright,
warm center. If you squint your eyes, all the
patterns seem to blur into a balanced mix of
red and green, florals and geometrics.

The walls and the woodwork are
glazed a deep loden green, with the
panels picked out in terra-cotta red to
create another layer of pattern. The
cornice is also painted red, almost
as if we were putting a bright ribbon
around the room. Notice the way the
bookcases are recessed into the
walls, which makes the shell of the
room simple and complex at the same
time. An Oriental rug, woven into an
abstract version of a garden, adds a
final layer of rich, dense pattern.

The library and this dining room were originally two separate rooms, but we took down the wall to create one larger, more inviting space. A seventeenth-century Spanish refectory table is surrounded by a set of the most amazing English Chippendale chairs owned by the client. Most people show off fancy furniture, but we went for a little mystery instead. You can still see their shape through the gauzy linen slipcovers, piped in red velvet, but the seriousness is taken down a notch. The table feels more relaxed. OPPOSITE: I think of chairs as sculpture, and this library ladder certainly qualifies. It's scaled so it can double as a seat. Notice how the feet curl up at the ends. The piece is a striking mix of red and black.

ABOVE: Millwork in a library doesn't have to be brown. We stained all the oak millwork in this room a dark green-black, which proved much more intriguing. Riding trophies and other objects are interspersed with the books on the shelves, to break up the mass of the bookcase. OPPOSITE: The wool cranberry-colored paisley on the wall warms up the room and seems to go along with the coffered ceiling. The two chairs are purposely in totally different styles to give more interest, but I covered them in the same wheat velvet to pull them together.

Why not show off your fabric? We turned this tree-of-life pattern into an architectural element by framing it with moldings and using it on a large scale. The sofa is upholstered in the same fabric, and the French chairs are covered in a striped velvet that picks up the colors. This room was done more than twenty years ago, and it still looks current today. Often the twist that feels foreign at first—like that panel on the wall—ends up keeping it fresh longer.

The meandering vines on the fabric seem to be echoed in the Chippendale-style gilt mirror, the Louis XV gilt bronze sconces, and the French tole and porcelain chandelier. All these foliate forms are based on nature, which seems appropriate in this winter garden room with limestone and sisal on the floor and French doors all around.

Even elaborate patterns become almost every- where.

I know it sounds crazy, but it's true. This eighteenth-century Montgolfier toile, inspired by the French brothers who invented the first practical hot-air balloon, seems to merge into the background. It wraps the room and actually feels very restful. The moldings were already taken out, and I needed to put something back in, so I effectively redrew the room by outlining it in black velvet ribbon. There's black velvet piping on the bed hangings and the chair, and a sunny yellow-and-black silk plaid offers a little contrast.

OPPOSITE: The handpainted Chinese silk wallpaper in this master bedroom was custom made in soft blues and grays and aged to give it an antique look. I picked up the colors in a trim on the lampshade and the headboard. The French doors are mirrored, to bring more light into the space.
ABOVE: Mirrored doors reappear in the bath, and the palette is in the same pale tones. I've always felt that a master bedroom and bath should have some relationship with each other.

Stripes are like architectural columns. They raise your eye.

Vertical stripes, in apple green silk and cream wool, make a small bedroom feel taller. The light hits those two fabrics in different ways, which gives another dimension to the pattern. The walls are upholstered in the same apple green and cream, but this time the pattern is a silk damask. All that beautiful fabric turns the room into a jewel box. The ruched ceiling on the canopy is called a "sky" in the world of design. How nice to lie in bed and look up at something so pretty.

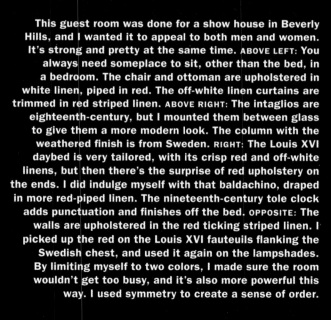

This guest room was done for a show house in Beverly Hills, and I wanted it to appeal to both men and women. It's strong and pretty at the same time. ABOVE LEFT: You always need someplace to sit, other than the bed, in a bedroom. The chair and ottoman are upholstered in white linen, piped in red. The off-white linen curtains are trimmed in red striped linen. ABOVE RIGHT: The intaglios are eighteenth-century, but I mounted them between glass to give them a more modern look. The column with the weathered finish is from Sweden. RIGHT: The Louis XVI daybed is very tailored, with its crisp red and off-white linens, but then there's the surprise of red upholstery on the ends. I did indulge myself with that baldachino, draped in more red-piped linen. The nineteenth-century tole clock adds punctuation and finishes off the bed. OPPOSITE: The walls are upholstered in the red ticking striped linen. I picked up the red on the Louis XVI fauteuils flanking the Swedish chest, and used it again on the lampshades. By limiting myself to two colors, I made sure the room wouldn't get too busy, and it's also more powerful this way. I used symmetry to create a sense of order.

ABOVE: When I found this toile with farm animals and Swiss chalets, I thought it would be perfect for a little boy's bedroom. Just for fun, I took a striped wallpaper in tan and cream and ran it horizontally around the room. It reminds me of a log cabin. OPPOSITE: Blue-and-white-striped cotton runs up the wall and hangs over the beds, to form a half-tester. The pattern on the wallpaper, a jungle scene with elephants, is strong enough to balance the stripes, which I turned on their side and used to trim the upholstered headboards.

A breakfast room is the kind of space where you can take a few risks, and the Fornasetti plates add a surreal edge. OPPOSITE: Nothing beats the graphic impact of a black-and-white stripe. Hang a Veuve Clicquot–yellow bulletin board with zigzagging black ribbon and a print by Jean-Michel Basquiat, and color becomes part of the pattern. A branch-shaped bronze candelabra is the finishing touch.

Be brave. Be bold. Playing

it safe gets you nowhere.

ABOVE: Vertical stripes in a laundry room turn horizontal in the powder room, and there's more black and white on the diamond-patterned vinyl floor. The paneled cabinet hides an old-fashioned pull-down ironing board. OPPOSITE: How can you warm up a stainless steel kitchen? The client had a bottle of Veuve Clicquot champagne on the counter, and that yellow label was the spark for this scheme. I lined the shelves in Veuve Clicquot–yellow flannel and used the same fabric on a window shade. That brilliant yellow, and the black-and-white stripes, connect it to the adjoining breakfast room.

The floor is yet another opportunity for pattern. This "pillowed" walnut parquet was inspired by a traditional French design. The Fortuny fabric on the chair is used on the wrong side, which makes it a little softer. OPPOSITE, TOP LEFT: In eighteenth-century France, where chairs were lined up against the wall until needed, the back of a chair was often upholstered in a less expensive fabric such as ticking or gingham. I like to carry on that tradition, simply because I enjoy the contrasting patterns. TOP RIGHT: Flowers bring life to a room. BELOW LEFT: All you need is one or two, and I'll tuck them anywhere I can. BELOW RIGHT: Everybody expects embroidery on silk, but not on ticking. I love to tweak our perceptions of high and low.

Passion, Discipl

Serene, *Cozy*, Wel

Dynamic, Laye

Pleasing, *Classic*, C

Rich, Juxtapo

Character, *Tranqui*

Functional, Clari

Natural, Sophistic

Enthusiasm, Calm

Generosity, Joy, Re

Peace, *Eleg*

ne, Beautiful,
coming, **Dazzling,**
red, Purposeful,
Composed, **Relaxed,**
sition, Mellow,
Personal, **Refined,**
y, *Contrast,* Grace,
ated, **Thoughtful,**
Power, Presence,
lief, *Contentment,*
nt, Gorgeous.

II. CHICAGO

Our home is all about family and friends.

The front door is painted a classic black and surrounded by flowers and shrubs. I like to have all that life around me as I come in.

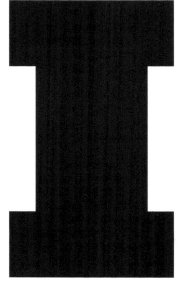

It was my father who first suggested I come to Chicago. He was a microbiologist doing research there and living in Lake Forest, which he thought might have an interesting college for me. So I enrolled. In Rome, I had been studying law, but in America, I switched to my first love, art history. And then I met the love of my life, Steve, who had grown up in Lake Bluff, and when we married Chicago became home.

I wanted to start my own business, so I opened a gallery, specializing in the antique prints I had always collected. But it wasn't the typical cool white box. My gallery was furnished with a sofa and chairs and the antiques I loved. It felt more like a living room, because that's the way galleries were in Europe. People came in for a print and stayed for hours. We sat on the sofa and we talked. Two years after that, a client asked me to design their house, and that's how my interior design business started.

We found our own home in a similarly serendipitous way. We were living in an apartment with three small children when a childhood friend told us about this townhouse, built by Potter Palmer in 1890, that was about to come on the market. Our friend lived two doors down with family and thought it would be a great place to raise children. We arranged to take a look, and as soon as we walked through the first floor and saw the garden and the coach house in the back, we were hooked. The children could open the back door and play outside on their own, safely. And they could walk to school, which was only three blocks away. I told my husband to overlook the plate-glass windows that didn't open and the laminate in the kitchen—marks of a misguided 1970s modernization. I knew I could make it beautiful again.

The first thing you see in our entrance hall is that bench, upholstered in a bright red, yellow, and black suzani. There's something playful and irreverent about it, which I like. There are no rules in decorating, and for me, the beauty is when you step outside the lines. The sisal runner on the stairs is durable and looks very smart bordered in black velvet. That's Greta, the rescue dog we adopted a year ago.

The townhouse template turned out to work very well for our family, because it allowed us to be together, yet apart. If you needed quiet, there was always a separate room on another floor. The layout is logical. As you walk in the front door, to the left is the kitchen, and beyond that, the library/family room, which opens to the garden. You go up one flight to the living room and a dining room. The master bedroom and another sitting room are on the third floor. And the fourth floor is the children's domain, with all their bedrooms.

When David Adler, an architect who designed some of the great American country houses, lived in our townhouse around 1910, he reworked the facade to move the entrance from the second floor to the first. He was the one who installed the beautiful eighteenth-century floor made of slate and marble in the entrance hall. I made my own changes, too. I added all the French doors, which have a great advantage over solid wood. They still let the light through even as they separate rooms. And if you don't want to see into the room, you can mirror them. A pair of mirrored French doors leads from the entrance hall to the kitchen.

The kitchen is the heart of the house. This is where we spend lots of time, where the children would do their homework, where we go through the mail. There's a big bulletin board on the wall with cards and notes and snapshots of the people in our lives, updated with the latest adventures and trips. I get to hear about everyone's day while the pasta is boiling. We often eat right here, on the old French farm table. My attitude toward furniture is simple: If it starts out already old, it will just keep getting better.

Next is the library. We love to read, and we like to keep our books around us. Even with all the bookcases in the house, you'll still see stacks of books in every room. They just seem to proliferate around us. In the library, we have built-in bookcases and paneled walls painted in a shadowy taupe that makes them look as if they have been here forever. I like to work in a corner by the window, sitting at a simple desk I designed that's modeled on an early Italian refectory table. A set of three pairs of French doors open to the garden. During the summer, we live outside. We eat breakfast, lunch, and dinner out on the terrace, which is very Italian and unusual in Chicago. When we have beautiful weather, I like to take full advantage of it.

Upstairs, on the second floor, I took down walls and basically eliminated the hallways to open up the living room and the dining room. I like the fact that you can see straight through the length of the house, which means both rooms are bathed in light as the sun moves from east to west during the day. Where the walls once stood, I installed old Corinthian columns. It's a little ironic to demolish a wall and then put up old-fashioned columns, but that's what I like about it. The new sense of expansiveness feels very contemporary, yet the columns reiterate the classical proportions and suit the style of the house.

When I began this project, I didn't set out with an overall concept for the décor. First you have to get the architecture right, then what's important to me is that each room has its own character. Yet none should overwhelm the whole. Many of the furnishings in the living room have followed me around for years. I bought the two Louis XVI–style Jansen bèrgeres with turned arms before Jansen became fashionable again. I've had the sofa since our first apartment and already recovered it twice. The Louis XVI chairs were bought at auction twenty-five years ago. Two people, or twenty, can be comfortable here. I designed a pair of banquettes for either side of the fireplace because they're a great way to take advantage of a space that's often unused. Besides, I tend to gravitate to the corners of a room. The fabrics are all in shades of cream and taupe and chocolate brown and red, with a touch of acid green to shake things up.

I picked up the cream and the chocolate brown and the red in the adjacent dining room. The walls are painted a warm Pompeian red and glazed in a crisscross pattern, which adds texture and depth and catches the light. Red is so much a part of my vocabulary. I couldn't do without it. People will often use it in a dining room, thinking that they can be more adventurous there since they're not in it for long stretches of time. There's also a theory that red makes you feel hungry, so it's very appropriate. And it's one of those colors that are even more beautiful at night, especially in candlelight.

The master bedroom is done in another favorite color, apple green. Years ago in London, I found a lovely apple green–and–cream toile that's a meandering fantasy of flowers and vines and little Chinamen with parasols by Pillement. I upholstered the walls with it and made it into window treatments, with a thick flannel lining to absorb the traffic noise from the street. I love the morning, and I like to put bedrooms on the east side of a house so people can wake up with the sun. When I see that apple green, it feels like springtime to me, even when there's snow outside. And if I can't fall asleep at night, I count flowers instead of sheep.

The colors make me happy, and every piece of furniture holds a memory. Wherever we have lived, I've always found a place for our favorite things. The colors may be a bit faded. The textures are not shiny and new. But these objects have stood the test of time. I've learned that if you just buy something to fill a space, it doesn't always follow you. You'll drop it along the way. So if I can't find exactly what I want, I will wait until I do. Those are the pieces you really love, and they become an integral part of your rooms. When the architecture, the shape, and the proportions are right, the room will show off whatever you put into it. For me, the greatest compliment is when people walk in and assume all the changes I made and the details I added are original. They can't believe it wasn't all here, always.

I'm so grateful for this house, because it has allowed us to fully enjoy the city. Here we are, right in the midst of downtown Chicago, yet we could open the back door and let the children play outside in our garden. We've had many broken windows from games of kickball, but who cares? We never felt we had to move away to find more room when they were little, and now that they're grown, we still have no intention of moving. We love our home.

It's the warmth

the living room, Venetian plaster walls add texture and depth and last forever—if it can survive Pompeii, it should be good enough for us. I chose raw silk for the curtains in the same creamy taupe as the walls and left it unlined so you can see the light shining through. A band of custom red and acid green trim along the leading edge accentuates the height of the windows and the simple, tied-back curves of the fabric. The floor is proper old-school rush matting, such as you might see in an English country house—great texture, very practical, and softer than sisal. I'm still looking for a console to go in between the windows, where I now have a large urn. The eighteenth-century Italian bracket just above it formerly belonged to interior designer Syrie Maugham and has great style.

that draws you in.

MIRRORS

After searching for years for just the right thing to go on either side of the fireplace, I finally found a pair of enormous eighteenth-century Swedish mirrors. Mirrors bring in more light and add another dimension—these are so large they almost feel like windows, which opens up the room even more. I took down the wall opposite the fireplace, and now you can see the stair hall, which is open to the living room, reflected in the mirror on the right. The mirrors were originally simply the giltwood portion, and then I added another frame, wrapped in chocolate brown silk velvet. It's an unexpected twist that makes the outline even bolder, adds a little more texture, and gives an antique piece an updated edge.

The fabrics in this room are all interrelated. Something that is used on one piece will often reappear somewhere else, which ties the space together in a subtle way. The banquettes on either side of the fireplace are upholstered in a pale cream linen velvet, with a bolster covered in red-and-cream ticking. The ticking reappears on the back of the Louis XVI fauteuils. I knew they would float and be moved wherever they were needed, and I wanted to make sure the back looked just as good as the front. The seat is covered in paisley—very unexpected on a French chair. The sofa is covered in linen damask, which looks raw rather than polished. Then there's the surprise of that acid green silk on the Jansen bergères.

Everyone looks wonderful in a red room. Your skin glows. An instant lift!

Yet another reason to use red in a dining room! As far as the table is concerned, I prefer a round shape rather than a rectangle. A round table is very democratic, and you can always squeeze in one more person. And if you put a skirt on the table, it really doesn't matter what's underneath. Fabric on the table and the chairs also has a softening effect on the room. Chocolate brown mohair velvet highlights the wonderful round backs of the Jansen chairs. The chandelier with alabaster cups was inspired by a fixture at the Villa Kerylos, a Greek villa reconstructed at the turn of the century on the Côte d'Azur. I picked up the classical motif with a Greek key border on the curtains.

I don't set a particularly fancy table, but I do love little accessories that add character. I've collected all sorts of silver salt cellars and mustard bowls, just for fun, over the years. That Italian candelabra in iron, hung with crystals, is one of my favorite pieces. It has such an unusual shape.
OPPOSITE: The Greek key pattern is appliquéd on the chocolate brown mohair velvet and outlined in red silk embroidery. I like the idea of taking a simple material like linen and adding something precious to it.

I love tartan. I like the clean, crisp geometry of the plaid and the unusual combinations of colors. I'm also entranced by the history of it—the fact that it can be traced as far back as the fifth century and that each pattern represents a particular Scottish clan. Wearing tartan is like showing your flag. It's a powerful symbol and a beautiful pattern, and it adds strength and warmth to any room.

Layers of color and pattern make the library feel cozy, and tartan is just the beginning. There's an English paisley on the sofa, and the rug is a patchwork, made up of bits and pieces of nineteenth and twentieth century rugs—very practical with children running in and out from the garden. The pillows are done in a Greek vintage fabric. Swing-arm lamps and branching candlesticks add that touch of black that I can't do without.

A room filled with books feels very comfortable to me.

Certain colors suit books, and red is one of them. I lined the bookshelves in red felt to pick up the red in the upholstery and add a little depth to the room. I like the lean lines of the desk and those delicate lyre-shaped legs—the desk doesn't block the light from the window. I'll sit in that chair, covered in a silk from Uzbekistan, and work happily for hours. The nearby nineteenth-century club chair, upholstered in a soft strie linen velvet in taupe, has a tall back and just the right curves, so you can pull the ottoman out and sit back with a book and read comfortably.

One wall in the library is covered in the same red felt I used for the interior of the bookcases, which makes the white nineteenth-century limestone fireplace really stand out and offers a bold break from all the paneling. Although the Dutch-style faux-tortoise frame with the mottled mirror looks old, it's actually new—we had it made. I had it set on a track so you can slide it to one side to reveal the TV. The Greek Chimera cup is a charming copy of an antique piece. OPPOSITE: I once had a client who looked at an ottoman and said, "Where am I going to put my drink?" So now I do concealed pullout trays on my ottomans. It's the best of both worlds—you can set down a gin and tonic and still put your feet up.

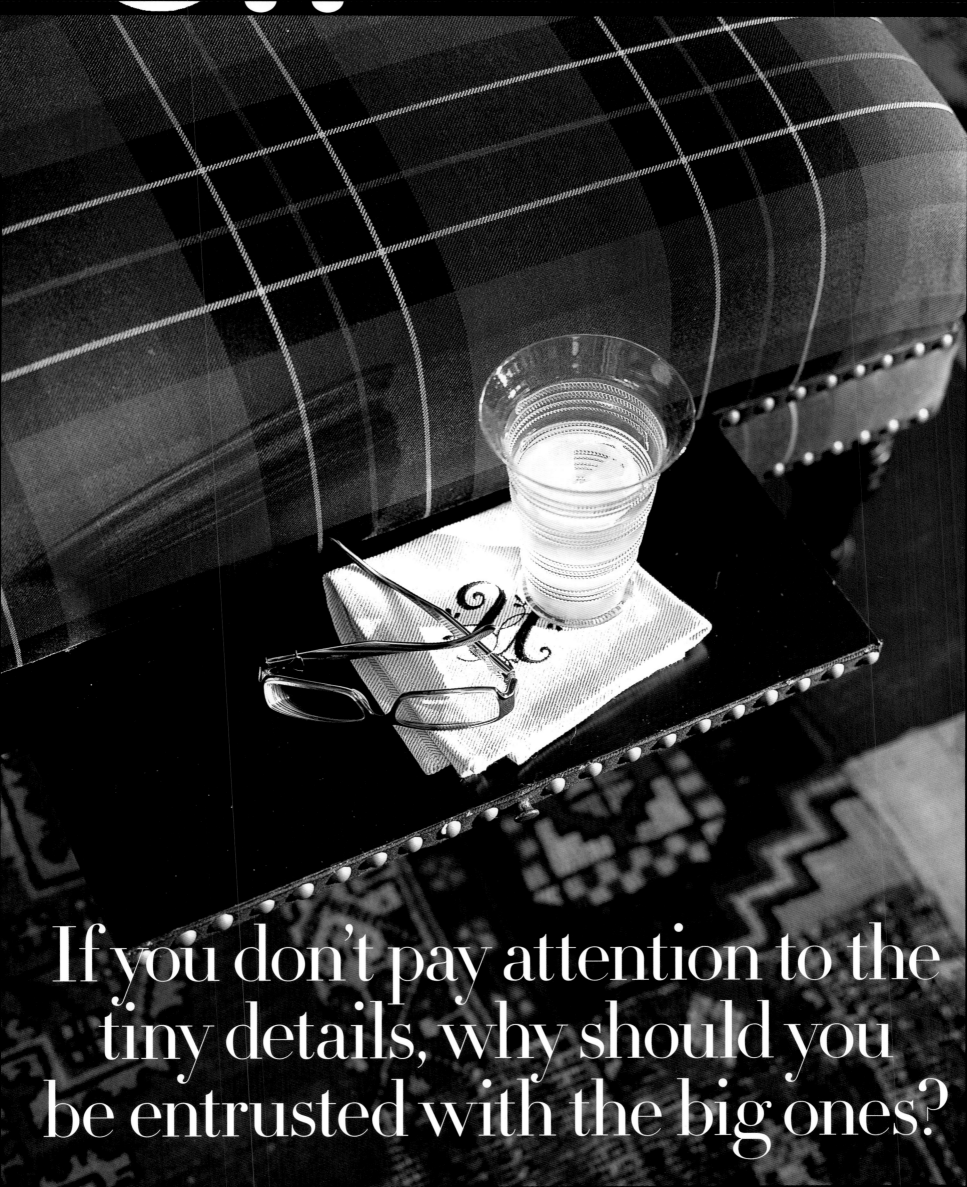

If you don't pay attention to the tiny details, why should you be entrusted with the big ones?

THE KITCHEN

I think of my kitchen as a working laboratory, and I wanted to keep it simple. This is the one place where I don't like a lot of color. I just wanted white marble and old wood. The French farm table is almost eight feet long, and lots of things happen here besides meals. I have files, as well as serving pieces, in the pullout drawers under the banquette, and I'll often do the household accounts at the table. I'm always thinking about how many ways I can use a room, and building in the things I need for various functions. Bookshelves under the window hold cookbooks, so all my recipes are within arm's reach.

I paired the old French farm table with modern stainless steel chairs. The ticking on the seat of the banquette is laminated, so it's easy for diners to slide in and out. I like banquettes because they feel more relaxed, and you can always fit in one more friend. In the evening, we dim the overhead lights, light some candles, and have a great relaxed dinner right here.

Just as I tried to make the most of every room, I designed the garden for multiple uses. The tree-shaded benches are great for reading. Limestone pavers work well for kickball—and we've had a few broken windows in the coach house at the far end of the garden. The table and banquette, just outside the back door, are where we eat all the time during the summer. It turns the backyard into our own little country house. OPPOSITE: When David Adler redesigned the front facade of the house to bring the entrance down to the ground floor, he added the Regency-inspired balcony. The knot garden in front plays on the same X-shaped pattern as in the railings.

ABOVE: The master bedroom walls are upholstered in an apple green–and–cream toile based on an eighteenth-century drawing by Jean-Baptiste Pillement. A custom scalloped-loop trim runs along the edge where it meets the wainscoting, which is painted in a faux-bamboo trellis pattern. I bought that Louis XVI chair out of the Jayne Wrightsman sale at Sotheby's, my very first "big piece."
OPPOSITE: The headboard, bed skirt, and table skirt are done in a contrasting silk plaid in the same colors. The table is topped with a Portuguese cutwork cloth in crisp white linen.

You can't do something that just looks pretty. It has to work.

The round Regency table, formerly owned by Bill Blass, represents the fanciful side of English furniture. It's like a wonderful piece of sculpture between the two club chairs, but it's also right where you need it, to set down a drink or a book.

The first thing I do in a room is look at the space and think about all the various things that people could do there. I'll ask my clients how many people they usually entertain at one time, to make sure we have enough seats in the living room to accommodate them. Do they like to have large cocktail parties? Then they'll need a certain amount of standing room as well. I also want to know how they plan to use the room when they're on their own. If they think they will sit there in the evenings, it's nice to orient the room toward the fireplace. But if they would like to be able to do some work on a Sunday afternoon, we might want to turn the focus around to a window and add some sort of desk. I'll often put a table behind a sofa, because it can double as a desk, a serving area for drinks, or even be turned into an informal place to have dinner. I always make an effort to create a room that encourages people to spend time there, bringing life to the space.

A floor plan should be flexible so it can adapt to different uses. The Italian word for furniture, *mobili*, is derived from the Latin word *mobilis*, which means "movable, quick". Furniture used to move around much more, before we were spoiled by central heating. In winter, you would sit on the south side of the house. In summer, you would move away from the light. I think one reason I love chairs so much is that you can easily pick them up and put them wherever you want. It's that change, and that hum of activity, that keeps a room alive.

The entrance to this long, rectangular living room is in one corner, which means you can't see such features as the fireplace from the doorway. So I had to create another focal point, with the games table and chairs, to give you something to look at as soon as you walk in. Two comfortable club chairs face one side of the double-sided sofa, to form a second seating area centered on the fireplace. The third is at the far end of the room. If you plan to float furniture in the middle of a room, as I did with those club chairs, make sure you like the way they look from the back.

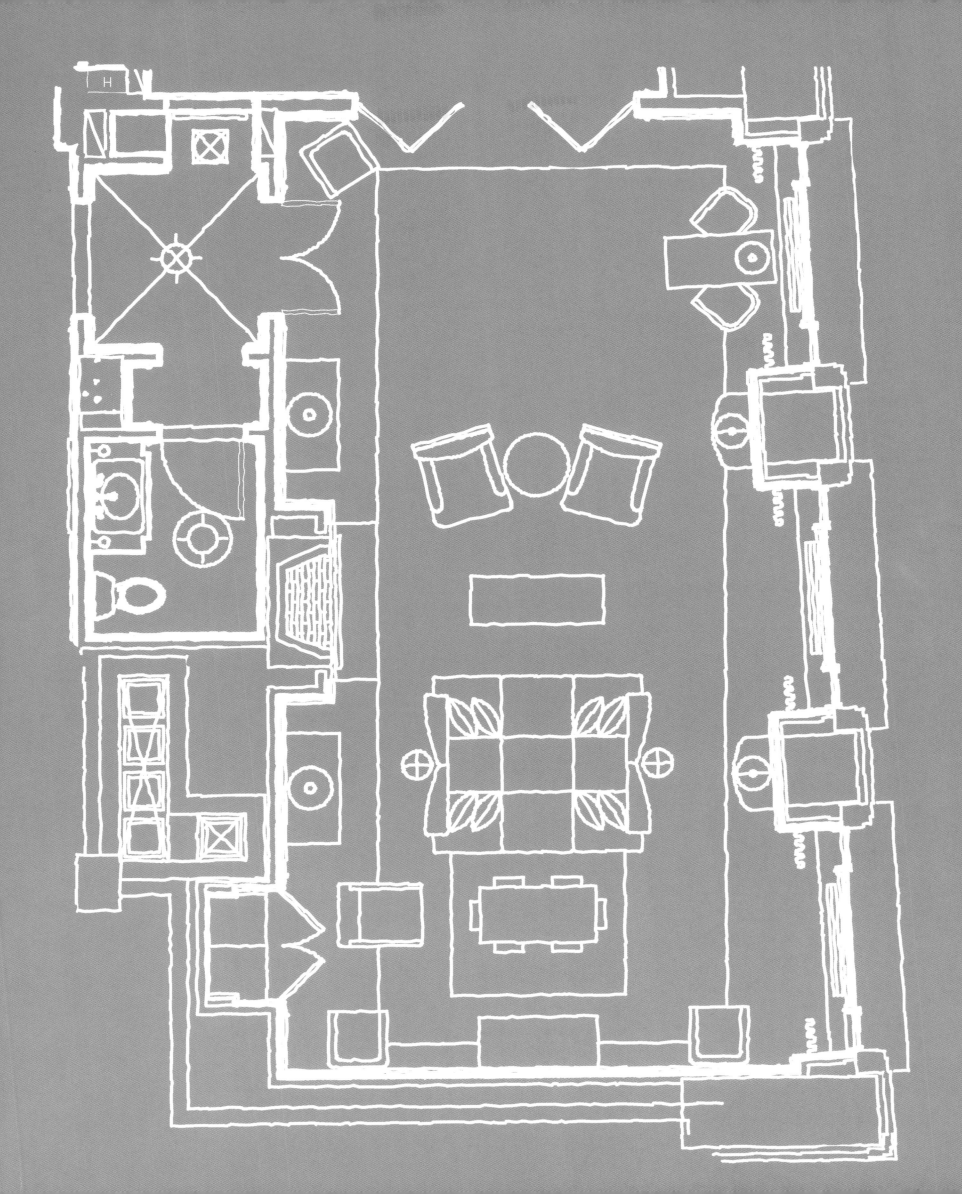

Painted Chinese panels turn the dining room into the living room's garden view.

The openness between the two rooms made me think of this space as a loft, but with classical instead of contemporary architecture. The living room was exceptionally long, with a fireplace in the middle of one long wall and windows on the other. I found a way to fit in three seating areas: one at the window with a games table, one at the fireplace with two chairs and a sofa, and one—with the other side of the double-sided sofa—in the foreground. The back-to-back sofa is a great way of seating more people without taking up too much space. We've been using those for over twenty-five years.

You have to consider how people are going to move through the room.

If I had done the typical setting with a sofa in front of the fireplace, flanked by two chairs, the sofa would have turned its back to the windows and blocked the view. This way, I have a more efficient seating arrangement—the other side of that double sofa faces a beautifully lacquered Chinese armoire—and a clear passage down the left side of the room to that third seating area.

I came up with an unusual palette for the handpainted Chinese wallpaper—taupe, hot pink, and turquoise blue—that is echoed in the Chinese export porcelain.

OPPOSITE: A raw linen scrim veils the 1940s crystal chandelier. You can still see the sparkle of the lights and the crystal, but it's more mysterious and sexy this way—like that famous photograph of Marilyn Monroe taken through a chiffon scarf. I think life is vastly improved with dimmers, so I install them on all the light fixtures in projects. Being able to control the light is essential if you want to create atmosphere.

The English Regency chair was bought from the Bill Blass sale at Sotheby's and stands alone, in all its glory, anchoring a corner of the living room. OPPOSITE, CLOCKWISE FROM TOP LEFT: The French eighteenth-century Louis XVI mahogany games table, with a pair of Louis XVI chairs, also works as a desk or a great place for two people to have an intimate dinner. A vase adds another turquoise blue accent. The sconces are dimmed down, to look like candles. A ceramic garden stool doubles as an end table.

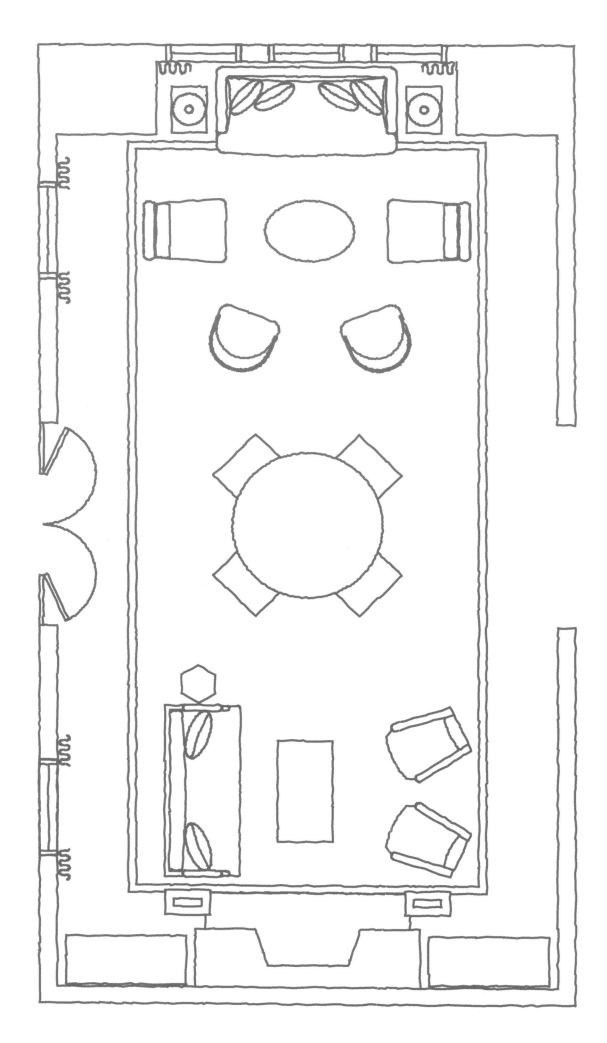

LEFT: I'll often use a big round table to center a room and spin it off in various directions. It creates a stopping point in the middle of this long, narrow living room. OPPOSITE: A center table is a great place to display books or set down a tray of cocktails, and I like to surround it with stools in the eighteenth-century way. They're small and versatile.

ABOVE: The fireplace side of the room is very cozy, with Jansen club chairs and a Louis XVI settee upholstered in rose-and-white ticking. The white woodwork and the painted wallpaper make it feel like a garden. OPPOSITE: A sunny corner at the other end is furnished with Gustavian painted chairs upholstered in a gray-and-white gingham check next to a slipper chair covered in gray silk and gray-and-white ticking. I love that mix of high and low. The tray table is so convenient—it can move anywhere.

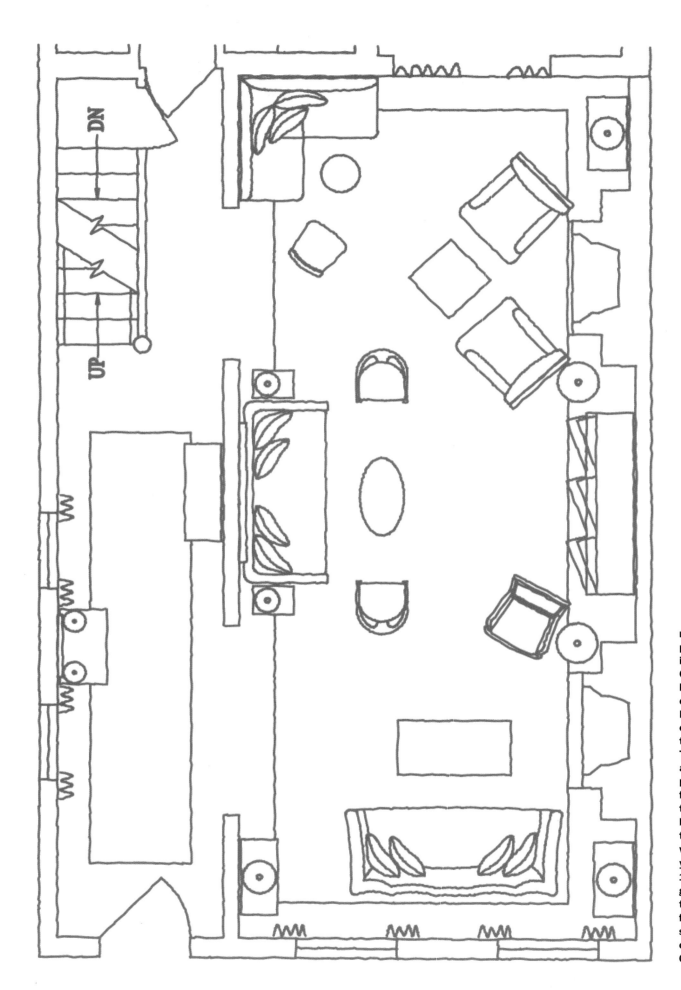

LEFT: A wall between the parlor and the dining room in this nineteenth-century Georgian-style townhouse had been taken down to create one long living room. In order to use all the space effectively, I broke it up into three distinct seating areas. The two at each end are anchored by the matched pair of Louis Seize limestone fireplaces, and the third, in the middle, faces a large bookcase. OPPOSITE: I unified the long room with that wonderful custom-made yellow wallpaper, based on a 1930s design. This seating group is centered around the fireplace. I covered the frame of the mirror in the same fine dark green velvet corduroy that I used on the Gustavian chair.

A large part of a space's success comes from the fluidity of the traffic patterns.

The flow is easier when you create several seating areas that can expand and contract. The chairs can move to be part of the group by the fireplace or the group centered on the large neoclassical bookcase. When choosing furniture, scale is always a consideration. In general, I think a sofa should not be more than two-thirds of the length of a wall, and a mantel should be no more than one-third the length of a wall, but these are guidelines, not hard-and-fast rules. I designed the simple Directoire-style stool, which is one of my mainstays. It can mix in anywhere and migrate wherever you need it. I love to do it in vintage or antique textiles so it is unique.

ABOVE LEFT: The camelback sofa creates a nice silhouette against the windows, and the boldly patterned damask plays off the wallpaper so beautifully. ABOVE RIGHT: A cozy banquette in a corner forms the third seating area and makes a great place for a quiet conversation. The meandering branches on the wallpaper lift the eye and make the room feel taller. RIGHT: The view from the living room into the entrance hall is focused on a neoclassical chest and a mirror, lit by two candlestick lamps and flanked by two stools. The symmetries reinforce this as a focal point. When I'm designing a house, I stand in the middle of each room and turn and study each view, imagining how I can make it the best it can be. When you look from one room to another, I want your eye to land on something interesting. OPPOSITE: The hand-painted wallpaper has a whimsical quality that softens and humanizes the traditional Georgian architecture of the room.

For me, comfort is the greatest luxury.

A big wide ottoman, large enough for a tray of drinks or a pile of books, practically says, "Put your feet up." It immediately sends a message—this is soft, not hard; relax and enjoy yourself. I added another layer to the stripe with velvet piping in a diagonal pattern and a nailhead trim.

y memories of growing up in Rome always start with a long table full of people— multigenerational, with friends and family and grandparents and children. Every meal was a reunion, with a big mix of personalities and lots of conversation; everyone lingered for hours. I also remember mellow, sunlit afternoons when I would sit with my grandmother in a quiet corner and talk with her while she knit—that must be where my fondness for corners comes from! She took very good care of her house, and I always wanted to help polish the silver or iron the linens. The satisfaction of curling up at night between freshly pressed linen sheets was even more intense when I learned to appreciate the effort that went into them.

A home is the sum total of all those daily rituals. If you start your day with a cup of Earl Grey tea, have it in your favorite cup. Sit down at a table where you can enjoy the morning sun. I want to celebrate each moment. Your home should feel special. In order to achieve that, you have to put the same energy into it as you hope to get back from it. I'm very particular about the objects that I let into my house. Everything has been chosen because it means something to me, and I think all that care and attention shows. A house requires a huge amount of love to turn it into a home.

Designing a home has a lot to do with generosity, and thinking of others. From the minute you walk into the entry, you should feel welcome. There should be somewhere to sit and take off your boots, a place to set down your keys, a mirror where people can

I want people to walk

perform a quick check coming and going. I've always wanted to do an entryway with a fireplace. Wouldn't that be wonderful? Then there's the living room. That term is often a complete oxymoron. It's not living, it's dead. Nobody wants to go into a room that feels stiff and formal. In my living room, nothing is too precious to be used. I believe in natural, forgiving fabrics that just get better with age, so you can lean back against the pillows and put your feet up on the sofa. Isn't that what we're all yearning for?

I can already hear that sigh of relief—finally, we're home. Now we can relax. The furniture is comfortable. There are always plenty of places to sit, a desk where you could write, a cozy spot to read. What's the point of a room where you have to worry about a child or a pet snuggling up to you on the sofa? That's one of the reasons I love slipcovers. They look even better after they have been washed a hundred times. The whole point of a living room should be to bring people together. Furnish it with the things you love. I have a number of things from my grandparents; they all carry so many memories. If you like needlepoint, find a great old chair covered in it or do your own needlepoint cover for a pillow. Home should be an expression of *you*.

After all, the most intimate thing you can share with friends is yourself. You want people to be comfortable when they come to see you. But comfort is not just about soft fabrics and luxurious details. You also have to be comfortable in your own skin. Then you will be happy in your rooms, and your friends will be, too. I've always thought, if you really want to get to know someone, just invite him over to eat in the kitchen! Come in, have a meal. Make yourself at home.

in and say, "Ahhhhh..."

WARMTH

Red and yellow is an unbeatable combination when you want to create warmth, and it becomes even richer when you start to layer on texture and pattern. A gingham check, a bright floral, vibrant stripes—they're all bright and cheerful. One pattern per fabric was not enough, so we had the gingham check overprinted with the floral, which makes it even cozier. And one pattern per chair would have been just too predictable, so we used two on each wing chair and matching ottoman. Juxtaposing two fabrics on the same piece feels a little more free and informal. Then it takes a hint of audacity to finish it all off with a boldly custom-striped rug. That kind of confidence, and the warm, sunny colors, makes for a lively room.

The mix of patterns is even more fun when you figure out how the gingham and the floral are interrelated. Then the vividly striped rug brings in a whole new element, leading you straight out the French doors to a large terrace. It's fascinating how pattern can work for, or against, the architecture of a room. To add a little interest to the ceiling, we created shallow coffers with moldings made of cerused oak and set them on a diagonal. Diagonals are dynamic and always make a space feel larger. And the warm colors give it a glow. Red is the accent that runs through the room. I used it on the skirted table and the pillows, and to pipe the cushions and trim the window treatments. A red throw is also ready and waiting when you want something warm around your shoulders while you're reading a book.

The window treatments, which we had printed in blue and gray and coral pink, are made of a wonderful floral based on a nineteenth-century document. The fabric warms up a large bedroom. The ottoman at the foot of the bed hides a pop-up TV, which swivels around so it can face either the bed or the club chairs. OPPOSITE: The half-tester somehow makes a twelve-foot ceiling feel cozy. When you're lying in bed, it's nice to look up at something interesting like that delicately hand-painted porcelain chandelier, which was custom made in Paris for me for this room.

I set this contemporary Chinese porcelain on top of a tall chest to finish off the shape with a softer, more interesting line. I love that beautiful crackled blue-gray glaze against the grasscloth walls and the dark mahogany. OPPOSITE: The client had wonderful fine English furniture, like this nineteenth-century mahogany bowfront chest. The chair is based on a traditional design, with a very restrained rolled arm. But tradition doesn't feel stuffy here. It's clean and edited.

ABOVE: Comfort has a lot to do with scale, and this French bergère is the perfect size—generous, without overdoing it. OPPOSITE: I think an entryway should be furnished with more than just a table. This Napoleon III corner banquette allows people to sit here and relax—it really becomes an extra room when the clients are having a party. The striped Irish wool runner leads your eye up the stairs and echoes the beige-on-beige-striped wallpaper.

The sitting room of this Victorian house had a huge beautiful bay, and we decided to turn it into the most comfortable seating area, with a big plump banquette upholstered in linen velvet. Linen velvet just gets better with age, and it's practically indestructible, making it a great choice for a family with children. The slipcover on the ottoman can easily be cleaned. The room is elegant and practical at the same time. I love those little red swing-arm lamps—they're the perfect punctuation.

ABOVE: The sofa is slipcovered in linen damask, which I washed before we used it. It takes away the sizing and makes it feel more relaxed. The plain linen window treatments are Italian-strung—which means they are made up of straight panels that drop down at night and simply pull back with a string during the day. I designed the lamps, which are like old apothecary jars and filled, as they used to do, with colored liquid. OPPOSITE: The strong lines of the English chest-on-chest are softened by the intricate japanning. I had a little fun with the button-back chairs, covering them in the kind of cotton that an upholsterer would normally use as lining. It's unexpected and informal. I love the deep blue glass on the Venetian sconces, which is a more intense version of the blue on the Chinese porcelain.

That Louis Philippe tub chair is a distinctive piece, the kind that can take a while to find. I always tell my clients to be patient and not try to buy everything right away. That would be like taking all of your family photos at once, and then they won't tug at your heart the way snapshots taken at different times and places will. Good things are worth waiting for.

LIGHTING

The secret of lighting is all in the mix. Each room should have a variety of lights, because you need different types of light for different uses. Overhead lighting gives you an all over light. In this family room, we used wall washers to wash the fireplace wall—a focal point—with light. But then I always like to counterbalance a modern fixture with something vintage, and we found a nineteenth-century copper lantern and hung it in the center of the room. Table or floor lamps are great for task lighting; they cast a lovely glow. Keep in mind that the shape of a shade can make a lamp look new or old. I have one basic guideline—the more elaborate the lamp, the simpler the shade. And don't forget dimmers: Controlling the light creates instant atmosphere.

This room had no detail when we started, so we had to create it. We built the coffers on the ceiling and did a modern version of a seventeenth-century mantel with an elegant bolection molding. The steel cabinets on either side of the fireplace originally had steel doors, which we took out and replaced with steel grating so you can see the books on the shelves, lined with ticking. I like the contrast of hard steel and soft fabric. I had the fabric on the sofas quilted, so they would feel like a big blanket, and I covered the ottoman in long-wearing linen velvet. The legs on the ottoman create their own pattern and have a great shape, which relates back to the banisters on the stairs.

The concept is that you can relax and lounge anywhere. That's very Roman.

LEFT: The sofa is covered in a quilted linen, which is very forgiving. You don't have to think twice about putting your feet up. OPPOSITE: A nineteenth-century Italian painted chest adds a little patina to the room. The lamp on top is made from a bronze vessel that looks as if was acquired back in the days when young men came of age and went on a Grand Tour of Europe. The nineteenth-century wing chair is still in its original leather, which is comfortably worn in.

ABOVE: That Bennison linen print on the walls and the pillows and the coverlet is as Edwardian as you can get, and it makes this bedroom feel charmingly old-fashioned. OPPOSITE: Then the art on the walls takes it into another century. I love that contrast. It adds a sharp, contemporary edge to all the coziness.

A dressing room is such a civilized concept. ABOVE: A 1940s Italian chandelier adds a little romance to the lady's dressing room, which is outfitted with mirrored closet doors and a makeup table. An eighteenth-century English side chair offers an elegant place to sit. OPPOSITE: The Napoleon III–style cabinetry in the gentleman's dressing room is equipped with pull-out shelves and telescoping hanging rods, to make getting ready for an event or packing for a trip easy.

Fresh, **Bold,** *Open,*
Radiant, *Simplici*
Tradition, *An*
Individual, **Un**
Whimsical, Chi
Considerate, *Adap*
Daring, Appropria
Expansive, **Fan**
Exquisite, *Entran*
Thrilling, Brilliar
Pretty, *Glowing*

Instinctive, **Happy,**

ty, Depth, *Fantasy,*

using, **Alive,**

ique, Surprising,

c, *Breathtaking,*

table, **Appealing,**

te, *Extraordinary,*

ciful, Irresistible,

ing, **Sumptuous,**

t, *Splendid,* **Fun,**

Vivid, Graphic.

III. NEW YORK

A challenging space can spark inventive solutions.

ew York is a city that runs on creativity. There is so much talent and art here that it continually inspires me—and also acts like a little nip at my heels to make sure I keep up and keep moving. I was spending so much time here for work that my husband and I decided it made sense to look for a pied-à-terre in the city.

The apartment I found, on the second floor of a small brownstone-type building, was a little challenging. It's shaped like a dumbbell, with basically one room in front and one room in back, and a long hallway in between. The front, with French windows overlooking the street, was easy to envision as the living room. That left the back room as the bedroom, but there was something odd about the space—it had a long, narrow extension off the back, eight feet wide and twenty-three feet long, which was originally described as a closet. As I was looking at it, I suddenly thought, what if I put a daybed along the long wall and make that the bedroom? Then I could use the bigger room as a study/library. I needed space to work more than I needed room to sleep. That decision was the key to the design, and it made me look at the whole apartment very differently. Necessity is the mother of invention.

We were not allowed to move walls, so the architecture had to stay the same. But we redid the surfaces, scraping off layers of paint and replacing them where they had been

Here's another guideline: The more sophisticated the fabric, the simpler you should treat it. The Fortuny fabric on the Italian chair is so beautiful that it needs no embellishment. The patterns on the fabric and on the Chinese armoire are both very strong, and even though they're completely different they still relate to each other.

removed. The wood floors were unattractive and none of them matched, so we ran sisal carpeting all the way through, unifying the space. The other big question was what to do with the long, skinny hallway. I could ignore it—paint it white and hope it would fade away—or I could try to have fun with it. My decision came easily—I lacquered it vermilion red and hung a series of architectural prints, including one on the jib doors.

The kitchen was a tiny square, literally the size of a closet, so I decided to treat it like an elegant little bar. I mirrored the backsplash to expand the impression of space and did the countertops in black stone, to add a little drama. I rarely cook in New York. We eat out or order in, but you always have to be able to make a good cup of coffee or a big bowl of pasta.

In the living room, I managed to fit in three separate furniture groupings and a skirted console against one wall, which works as another unobtrusive desk. My daughter, Anna Lucia, likes to lie back and read on the nineteenth-century banquette, done in the style of Louis XVI, by the window. Opposite it is a slipper chair, which can be turned around to face the sofa, if needed. That group is on one side of the fireplace. On the other, it's balanced by a new corner banquette with a coffee table and two Regency spoon-back chairs, where we'll sometimes sit and have an informal dinner.

A red-lacquered Chinese armoire holds dishes, glassware, and napkins. The third seating area is centered around the sofa, which has a fancifully curved Venetian-style back and is upholstered in a wheat-colored linen velvet. I am addicted to linen velvet, first for its beauty—it's cut in such a way that the nap is irregular, and that's what catches the light and gives it such luster—and then for its practicality—you can wipe it and even scrub it, and it just gets better with age.

Behind the sofa is an eight-panel floor-to-ceiling eighteenth-century lacquered screen with a gilt pattern. I have a particular fondness for screens. They break up a flat wall and give a room a story and a narrative, just like a painting. But a screen is architectural in scale, so the impact is even greater. This screen has a beautiful design—none of the little scenes repeat themselves. It adds a whole other layer of exoticism.

The color scheme in the living room is wheat and cream, with accents of red and black. For some reason, I keep coming back to red and black. Red is passion and joy, but black is more sobering—it gives a room depth and history and age, bringing the room back down to earth. The combination of the two colors is very powerful.

In the study, I switched to paprika, a deep tone of orange. The sofa is slipcovered in a deep

Dutch blue corduroy, and it opens into a bed. So does the sofa in the living room, which means we can easily sleep six if we need to. I do my work in here, at an antique table I use as a desk. One wall is lined in bookcases and holds the television. It also holds my filing system, which consists of wicker baskets. I'm always in the midst of several jobs in New York, and every client is assigned two baskets. One is for fabric samples, floor plans, and snapshots of suggested furniture, with watercolor renderings of each room. The other holds construction drawings, with samples of hardware, finishes, and millwork. I like baskets because they are portable. You can carry them from the desk to a conference room or out to the job site. And when you put them back on the shelves, they still look very neat and clean. They're a great organizing tool, and they eliminate a lot of visual clutter.

Clients don't always believe me at first when I tell them this, but sometimes a small room can end up being the best room in the house. It certainly worked here. The bedroom, in that long, narrow space, is like a cozy cocoon. I upholstered the walls in red-and-white ticking, so it feels very cheerful and warm, and I covered the daybed in chocolate brown velvet. I also did a chocolate brown wainscoting and a chocolate brown horizontal stripe along the cornice, to widen a disproportionately tall space.

And somehow I fit in a drop-front chest at one end of the bed and a Louis XVI mahogany desk at the other. I can't seem to do a room without a desk. I think you should always have a place to read and write. It gives you yet another reason to be in the room. When my family is here, or my assistants are traveling with me, we can all find our own little corner.

The design makes use of every square inch, in multiple ways. The study magically turns into a dining room when we open up a drop-leaf table in front of the sofa and pull over a few chairs. Each room is very versatile. The apartment works as my second office and also as our weekend getaway when Steve and I want a fix of New York culture. There are five major museums within walking distance, or we can head over to Broadway for a play or Lincoln Center for a concert. Our children love to stay here as well, and they will bring their friends. My son Alex bought a Weber grill at the hardware store for the garden the first summer we were here.

For me, it's refreshing to get out of my daily routine and hit the ground running in another city. I like to see clients and friends and make the rounds of the auction houses and the galleries. So many people live with their eyes wide shut, but I am looking all the time. If you don't step out of your box, it's hard to keep growing and evolving. New York is invigorating to me.

Shots of red and black add drama to a neutral backdrop.

Decorating a room is a little like making a pasta sauce—you have to balance the furnishings just as you would balance the flavors. Most people would have hung similar paintings on either side of the fireplace, but I balanced a nine-piece watercolor by my mother, with one framed collection of intaglios. There are also sofas on either side, but one is a banquette that wraps the corner and the other is done in the style of Louis XVI. Yet both furniture groups seem to have equal weight. The palette of red and cream and taupe holds the room together, and then there is that strong note of black in the two spoon-back chairs, trimmed in nail heads that accentuate their curves.

I collected these wonderful old glass apothecary jars and put them on top of the nineteenth-century Chinese armoire. They add great scale and create a whimsical, eye-catching vignette with that African feather hat propped behind them. OPPOSITE: I love how my mother, an accomplished artist, did this watercolor of a dogwood tree in nine separate pieces, as though you were looking at it through a window.

The window treatments are made of plain silk, unlined and Italian-strung—no frills, very simple, with bamboo shades. I love the combination of silk and bamboo. OPPOSITE: I found that nineteenth-century giltwood clock at a flea market and liked the elaborate detailing. It's flanked by sculptures made by a Sicilian friend out of sea urchin shells and branches painted to look like coral.

Once again, you have to think of an interior like a painting, and build up the layers of color and pattern. The paisley on the lampshades adds another top note of red to the underlying blacks, golds, and creams.

ABOVE: I love the juxtaposition of raw steel and a traditional tartan wool in the study. The nineteenth-century French steel armoire holds things like stationery, light bulbs, and my tool kit. I used the tartan fabric on a diagonal on the chair, to kick it up. OPPOSITE: I put the rug on a diagonal, too, which energizes the room. The bookshelves, painted red inside, are done in two depths—twenty-four inches and twelve inches—to accommodate books and objects. It also lets me play with interesting arrangements of objects in front of the books.

ABOVE: This is the sofa in the study as it usually looks, with an ottoman upholstered in a bright suzani. OPPOSITE: When we want to have dinner here, we set the ottoman aside and pull out this nineteenth-century English mahogany table. The framed collection of tiny hourglasses is hung on a barely visible jib door that opens to a closet. Swing-arm lamps with paprika-red velvet shades also make this sofa a great place to read.

The half-tester over the daybed catches the eye and breaks up the length of the room. The same ticking that's on the walls is used on the pillows on the bed, but turned into concentric stripes this time. OPPOSITE TOP LEFT: A club chair by the window and a drop-front chest under a bulletin board create another spot to read or work. TOP RIGHT: A nineteenth-century French tole clock hangs in the center of the half-tester. BOTTOM RIGHT: More pattern—the mirror over the bedside desk has a paisley-covered frame. BOTTOM LEFT: And more color—roses add another red note.

I like to give new spin to old things.

What could be more classic than a blue-and-white toile? Then I mixed it up with acid green on the pillows and the throw. It changes your whole impression of this bedroom and gives it an updated feel.

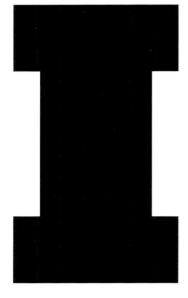love classical architecture and design. In Rome, I grew up with it. I know it so well and I appreciate it—which is why I can design a room that has all those pleasing qualities of symmetry and proportion—and then I like to give it a little twist. That twist is what takes it forward and makes it vital and current and fresh for today.

The twist can come in various ways. I happen to love seventeenth- and eighteenth-century furniture, but that doesn't mean I design eighteenth-century interiors. In my rooms, antiques rub shoulders with contemporary pieces, and the unexpected juxtapositions set off little detonations of delight. I will often mix elegant and casual, high and low, and do something like covering fine Chippendale furniture in ordinary muslin. I love the freedom that represents and the atmosphere it creates. It's confident and irreverent.

This is how style changes and design evolves. It's my way of propelling myself into the future. Make it young. Make it new.

It's very unexpected to cover the walls in this study in a Georgetown house with felt, but it gives me a deep, dark blue that you just can't get with paint. And it's a twist on the traditional dark paneling. I wanted something other than the standard-issue tartan, and I chose this one because it's so graphic. It looks almost modern.

The nineteenth-century English writing table in the corner is turned on an angle, which makes the room more dynamic. A trundle bed pulls out from underneath the sofa, allowing this study to double as a guest room. I love the brass accents and the way the white fireplace stands out against the blue felt. Soldier andirons are a jaunty finishing touch.

I like to take something staid

and proper and have fun with i

It's fun to pull out the fine china and crystal for a party—or even an intimate dinner for two—but to keep the table from looking too formal, instead of candles in classic white, try orange. It's a surprise to see them in the silver candelabra. And I like the exuberance of a big bunch of a single type of flowers in one color, like these orange tulips, instead of a more formal mixed arrangement, something anyone can do.

The table is beautifully set with gleaming silver, china, and crystal—and crisply ironed linen napkins. It shows your guests how much you care. Just pour the wine and let the conversation flow.

The organdy tablecloth has a lovely transparency. OPPOSITE: What could be more classical than a black-and-white marble floor? Then we shook things up with yellow silk window treatments, trimmed in orange velvet. The valence looks like daisy petals made of bright yellow silk. The hand-printed Hindustan paper by Zuber adds another touch of fantasy.

Most pool houses are merely a changing room, a bathroom, and a closet. But I turned this one into a pavilion where one could eat or lounge or read or entertain. The colors are rich and vibrant, but what really makes the room interesting is scale. Everything is big, even the oversized paisley pattern on the walls. The room is oddly shaped, with various angles, and instead of trying to hide them, I covered them in fabric and outlined them in blue velvet.

Since the pool house is in Southampton near the beach, I chose a blue-and-white palette and spiced it up with coral accents. Big blue banquettes add more seating room in two corners. The sisal carpet is woven in a wave pattern that reminds me of the sea.

A traditional chandelier, encased in sheer white scrim, becomes modern and mysterious.

I wanted to do something different with the chandelier. I had a vision of a Roman palazzo, with the furniture swathed in sheets and the crystal chandeliers protected with dust covers. They used to do that when the family went away for the summer. So I made my own version out of sheer white scrim. There's something very enticing about an object only half-seen—a secret fashion designers have known for ages. You can still see the chandelier, but somehow its solid bronze form has become as insubstantial as the gauze through which it is viewed. I call it my "ghost."

The Gustavian painted chairs are covered in coral linen with a white trim. OPPOSITE TOP LEFT: Instead of window treatments, we did portieres at the doors. TOP RIGHT: The centerpiece on the table is a simple pile of shells. BOTTOM RIGHT: The japanned bookcases add their own delicate pattern. BOTTOM LEFT: Window frames are outlined in blue velvet.

Symmetry creates order and calm, but every once in a while you have to break it.

Instead of two matching tables on either side of the sofa, one is skirted and the other is actually a chest. And there's only one red barrel table beside the club chairs. The chairs are upholstered in a linen damask turned inside out, to make the colors even softer. I had the walls overpainted in another damask pattern to add more texture to the room. A pair of 1930s faux-bamboo benches, covered in leopard-patterned silk velvet, are chic and versatile.

SPREZZATURA

Sprezzatura is an Italian word that means a certain nonchalance, a gift for making something that actually required a lot of effort look absolutely effortless. It's a charming quality and very Italian, and I like to think my rooms have a bit of it. That silk window treatment looks as if it were just casually tossed over the rod, but of course it's not quite so simple. Those swags do not automatically hang so perfectly. The fanciful sconce in the corner looks as if it had been there forever, but it took months to find.

The window treatments are made out of a tartan plaid, but in silk instead of the usual wool and in very unexpected colors. The clients already owned the Diego Giacometti coffee table, which was inspired by a classical Greek design. The chair in the corner is an updated version of a wing chair, upholstered in one of my favorite cut-velvet fabrics. I can't resist that zigzag.

Yellow, when it's combined with black, suddenly looks very sophisticated. OPPOSITE: The tester with a traditional coronet top feels much more modern when it's done in a bold stripe. I played with other graphic combinations of the same yellow, black, and white on the pillows. The coffee table is actually a 1940s bench made of metal and upholstered in black velvet.

This is a new, uptown version of an old country kitchen.

LEFT: The cabinets are done in cerused oak, with an old-fashioned blue-and-white gingham behind the glass doors. Honed Absolute Black granite on the island and countertops picks up the color of the ebonized beams and the floor and gives the kitchen a contemporary edge.
OPPOSITE: The banquette by the old refectory table is twelve feet long and laminated on the seat, to make it easy for diners to slide in and out. The Louis XIV–style chairs were updated with white paint. The kitchen is large, but it's amazing how intimate it feels.

A room lined with books does not have to look heavy.

The trick is in the shelves, which are open in back and on the sides. The cushions on the wraparound sofa are finished with Turkish corners, which make it feel like a big bed. A convenient running shelf just behind the sofa holds drinks when everyone gathers to watch a movie. An old-fashioned pelmet, reimagined in a more graphic way, frames the window.

I love cerused, or limed, oak. It's a finish developed by the renowned French designer Jean-Michel Frank and involves opening up the grain of the wood and rubbing it with lime, white paint, or putty. It stays in the crevices and brings out the pattern. Cerusing was very popular in the 1930s, and it still looks chic today. I think it gives the cabinetry in this kitchen a soft, mellow look.

I love threes, and this trio of hanging lights over the island has great iron shades. The hood over the stainless steel range is hidden in a chimneypiece that suggests an old-fashioned hearth. The glass on the cabinets is backed in a linen scrim, so you don't have to worry about how everything looks inside.

OPPOSITE: The client didn't want a conventional chandelier over the dining table, so I found this crystal ship instead. It's a whimsical gesture that completely transforms the room. The chairs are slipcovered in an embroidered print. ABOVE: Here's the more formal version of the room, without the slipcovers. The walls are covered in paper, hand-printed in a damask pattern, and then waxed. If Fortuny had ever made wallpaper, this is what it would have looked like.

I'll always find more than one reason to use a room.

A hall leading to the children's playroom becomes a showcase for their work, with blackboards alternating with bulletin boards. I even installed spotlights on the ceiling, just like in a real gallery.

People can always tell whether a room is lived in or not. We all know those living rooms that might as well have a rope at the entrance and a sign saying, "Look, but do not touch." Then there are those houses where nobody ever goes in through the front door, but instead come in from the back. I get a little sad when I look at those pristine, empty foyers. I tell my clients, "Let's do something different, and make the front entrance feel like somebody really lives here. Let's put up some hooks and hang up your straw hats and some of that fishing gear. What about a bench underneath, to take off your boots, and a big basket on a table to collect the mail?" I want to walk into a house and feel like someone's home.

If you put a sofa and two chairs in the living room and call it quits, it can end up looking like a hotel suite. You have to add that final layer of personal accessories, and then move them around occasionally. If you never change things, the room will become stale. I like to pick up the rugs in the summer and put slipcovers on the furniture. It's refreshing and makes it feel like a whole new space. A house is exactly like a garden. If you don't tend to it regularly, it dies. Every year in my own house, I take everything out of each room and clean it thoroughly, just like my grandmother used to do in Rome. Then I put things back in, but not necessarily in the same way. Some pieces may move to other rooms. I'm constantly rearranging. When I'm designing a house with clients, I try to get them to

The more a room is used,

think not only about what they need right now, but also about what they will want later—very much like a business plan. What will be happening in five or ten years in this house? How do they envision living in these rooms once the children are off at college?

Back at my desk, I fill my mind with images of the clients and their preferences, and then I focus on each room. If I haven't found more than one reason to be in a specific space, then I haven't done my job. Multitasking is a way of giving a room more value. For example, let's take the dining room. If you're only going to use it once or twice a year, then let's rethink that room. What about lining it with bookcases and turning it into a library? You can still have a big table in the center, where you could have a dinner party when you want to. But during the rest of the time the room won't languish; it will be used.

It was really a Victorian concept, to have a specific room devoted to each activity. If you were wealthy enough, you had a sitting room and a sewing room and a billiard room—all of a sudden everything and everybody was separated. All those various rooms were a sign of gentility in an English house. But in an old Italian palazzo, the spaces were larger and more communal. Many things happened in the same room. That's the way I prefer to live. In our library, my husband can be reading and I can be drawing at the desk, and we don't have to be talking, but we're still together. That feeling of community is one of the best things about a family, and a house.

the more wonderful it feels.

CHANGE

I have a theory about children's rooms. I think they should be able to grow up along with the child. That means that the fundamentals of the space—the bed, the chair, the desk—should not be juvenile. Invest in pieces that can adapt. You should be able to take the canopy off the bed when your daughter decides that she's too sophisticated for it. If the chair is comfortable and well made, it will be worth reupholstering when she declares that a sweet floral print is no longer acceptable. If your son wants to follow the latest trend, let him do it with accessories. Then, when it's over, you won't have a qualm about tossing them out or passing them on. The room should be able to evolve as their tastes change.

This playroom was designed for a boy and a girl, but it's also a great hangout space for the whole family to get together and watch a movie. The children can color or have a little snack at the table or play a game on the floor. The built-in bookcases are fitted with two separate desks. In the closet, the shelves are stocked with colored paper and glitter and glue, but that can change to typing paper and note cards when the children grow older. The biggest jolt of color is really in the carpeting. Take it away and you could have a neutral room, once you re-cover the ottoman. The walls are covered in a vinylized grasscloth, which is easily wiped down.

When I was asked to redesign a two-bedroom suite at the Peninsula Hotel in Beverly Hills, I knew it had to be all things to all people. Some come to relax, so the living room is great for lounging or dining or watching a movie. Others come to work, so there's a good-sized table for a business meeting and a pullout desk in a bookcase.

A screen covered in antiqued mirror adds a touch of Hollywood glamour, and it also expands the perception of space. The sofa is my own design; it's covered in a two-tone linen stripe in light, California colors.

A pedestal table in the center of the living room works for dining or an impromptu meeting. You can pull up any of the nearby armchairs and sit and be comfortable. But for a quick look at a book or a casual chat, the stools are right there and very unobtrusive. The French doors on the right open to a terrace.

ABOVE: The comfortable club chairs are upholstered in a soft cashmere paisley and can be turned around to face the TV, which is hidden behind doors in the bookcase. Red linen on the doors and lining the shelves adds a bright note. OPPOSITE: I hung a series of magnolia watercolors by my mother over the console to give this side of the room a focal point. The walls are covered in a patterned grasscloth, which adds texture and depth.

The canopy bed is made of raw steel, with linen damask bed hangings tied on the old-fashioned way. All that voluptuous fabric turns the bed into an inner sanctum. I put a desk right next to it, instead of the typical night table. It allows you to work in this room, if you want to. OPPOSITE: The armoire opposite the bed conceals a TV, and the antiqued mirror makes it feel less substantial.

A bedroom should feel

like a lush, private retreat.

ABOVE: The vanity, in dark wood and white marble, has a traditional look—and enough surface area to accommodate all your toiletries. OPPOSITE: I believe that baths should be very simple. Mosaic tile is about as decorative as I get. Then you can indulge, if you like, in beautiful linens. I managed to tuck in a dressing table between the bedroom and the bath.

I love a tented room. It immediately says that something fun is about to happen here. This playroom was originally a terrace, which was then enclosed. It's saturated with sunlight, which is another reason the tent effect made so much sense. You can pull some of the canvas window treatments shut when it gets too bright, or close them all completely when you want to watch a movie. A screen pulls down from the ceiling at one end of the room.

The white vinyl floor is a great surface for almost any game, and it's practically indestructible. The chairs and table can be replaced with real desks once the children get older. Toys and project supplies are organized in baskets and boxes on the bookshelves.

There
used to be
a crib
under that
canopy,
but now it
accents a
handsome
sleigh bed.

The room is growing up with its owner.
In the next phase, the toys and bears
will be removed, but I hope he keeps
those tin Napoleonic hats, turned
into sconces. His great-grandmother
needlepointed the rug with the drum,
and we borrowed the drum motif for
the shades on the standing lamps.
Military prints are framed in red,
white, and blue, and red grosgrain
ribbon gives the room a crisp outline.

CONCLUSION

Whenall is said and done, all that matters is that I want you to love your house. Even more importantly, your house must be a HOME. All of this effort to make each room beautiful is not really about me. It's about the people who live there. What I do is set the stage for people to enjoy their lives. I introduce clients to various concepts and then try to find the particular combination that suits them. The more open to new ideas a client is, the more I am excited by a project. The more challenging the site or structure, the more I learn and grow. But with all that, it takes a great relationship based on very sound principles of trust, faith, support, and some chance. When I walk away, I want to be sure that my client got more from the process than just some furniture and a pretty house. The greatest compliment ever paid to me, which I have received many, many times, is that the clients tell me they don't want to leave their home because they are so happy in it. What more could one want?

Working as a designer is a bit like being a portrait artist. The home needs to reflect the people living there, and if it doesn't, I have failed no matter how beautiful it may look. I'm always asking myself, Does this house capture the person? Will it work for all the life that is going to take place inside of it, with children and grandchildren and dogs?

I want people to love who they are and where they are and be happy with what they have. A home is not really about dramatic architecture or elaborate furnishings or the handmade trim on a curtain—although I admit I can obsess about any and all of those wonderful details. A home is about the people who share it with you. For me, home is my children, my husband, my family, and our friends. That is my life, and in the end, those people are ALL that matter!

Some people will arrange a few objects on the mantel and leave them there forever in a perpetual still life. I like to keep changing things around. I think it makes the room feel more alive. Here, two gilded porcelain French Empire cachepots on my mantel are filled with roses that I bought at Costco. It doesn't take much to make me happy.

RESOURCES & REFERENCES

Just a few of my favorite things in life

ROAMIN' ROME

Crocianelli—*for the best finishing touches and trimmings*
Via dei Prefetti, 37/40 00186
Rome

Di Castro—*beautiful antique Italian furniture*
Via del Babuino, 71 and Piazza di
Spagna, 5
Rome
www.dicastro.com

Dal Bolognese—*the best, and a gorgeous eighteenth-century location to boot*
1 Piazza del Popolo
Rome

Pierluigi—*my favorite neighborhood haunt*
Piazza de'Ricci, 144
Rome

Nino—*has been my standby for lunch in the shopping district for over 40 years*
Via Borgognona, 11
Rome

Da Lucia—*a very down-home hosteria in the heart of Trastevere*
Vicolo del Mattonato, 2
Rome

Gusto—*Hip and cool with delicious food and a view of Augustus' tomb*
Piazza Augusto Imperatore, 9
Rome

Raphael Terrace—*for the most incredible sunsets in Rome, drinks and/or dinner*
Raphael Hotel
Largo Febo, 2 (Piazza Navona)
Rome
www.raphaelhotel.com

Sant' Eustachio—*the VERY best in Rome for coffee and cornetto*
Piazza di Sant'Eustachio
Rome
www.santeustachioilcaffe.it

Montemartini—*the best in classical sculpture displayed in the first power plant in Rome*
Via Ostiense, 106
Rome
www.centralemontemartini.org

Palazzo Altemps—*a beautiful renaissance Palazzo that houses a wonderful selection of Rome's classical sculpture*
Piazza di Sant'Apollinare, 44
Rome

Palazzo dei Conservatori—*Michelangelo's amazing architecture*
Piazza Campidoglio, 55
Rome

Piazza Farnese (and Palazzo Farnese)—*sit at the cafe as it is perfect for drinks and to view the Carracci frescoes in the early evening as the sun is going down*
Piazza Farnese
Rome

La Farnesina—*a renaissance architectural jewel*
Via della Lungara
Rome

Botanic Gardens—*where we stroll and marvel at nature after we've enjoyed so much art and architecture*
Largo Cristina di Svezia, 24
Rome

Palazzo Spada—*another intimate palazzo with an amazing collection of paintings*
Piazza Capo di Ferro, 13
Rome

FINDING THE CHIC IN CHICAGO

David Adler homes—*finest example of residential architecture in Chicago and the North Shore*
The David Adler Music and Arts Center
1700 North Milwaukee Avenue
Libertyville, IL 60048
www.adlercenter.org

Richard Norton—*beautiful continental furniture*
Richard Norton Inc.
222 Merchandise Mart Plaza
Suite 612
Chicago, IL 60654
www.richardnortoninc.com

RL (Ralph Lauren restaurant)—*best lobster bisque in the city*
115 East Chicago Avenue
Chicago, IL 60611
www.rlrestaurant.com

Table 52—*one of my favorite neighborhood spots, great southern fare*
52 West Elm Street
Chicago, IL 60610
www.tablefifty-two.com

Follia—*best authentic Italian pizzas in Chicago*
953 West Fulton Market
Chicago, IL 60614
www.folliachicago.com

Alinea—*for a truly amazing culinary experience*
1723 North Halsted
Chicago, IL 60614
www.alinea-restaurant.com

Sweet Mandy B's—*best cupcakes in Chicago*
1208 West Webster Avenue
Chicago, IL 60614

Lyric Opera—*one of my favorite ways to spend an evening; considered one of the top opera companies in the world*
20 N. Wacker Drive, #860
Chicago, IL 60606
www.lyricopera.org

Museum of Contemporary Art—*a lovely way to spend an afternoon*
220 East Chicago Avenue
Chicago, IL 60611
www.mcachicago.org

Millennium Park—*wonderful gardens and sculpture*
55 North Michigan Avenue
Chicago, IL 60611
www.millenniumpark.org

Architectural boat tour—*an excellent way to experience the city and its architecture*
Chicago Architecture Foundation
224 South Michigan Avenue, #116
Chicago, IL 60604
www.architecture.org/tours.aspx

New Renzo Piano Wing (The Modern Wing) at the Art Institute of Chicago—*a wonderful place to enjoy the art within as well as experience its architecture*
Art Institute of Chicago
111 South Michigan Avenue
Chicago, IL 60603
www.artic.edu/aic

NEVER OLD IN NEW YORK

Luther—*exquisite antiques*
35 East 76th Street
New York, NY 10021
www.hmluther.com

Berndt Goeckler—*great eighteenth-century antiques mixed with 1930s to 1960s*
30 East 10th Street
New York, NY 10003
www.bgoecklerantiques.com

R. Louis Bofferding—*the chicest eye in the business*
970 Lexington Avenue (between 70th and 71st streets)
New York, NY 10021

Evergreen—*one of my picks for Northern European neoclassical furniture*
1249 Third Avenue (at 72nd Street)
New York, NY 10021
www.evergreenantiques.com

Amy Perlin—*a warm and fantastic dealer of everything that is beautiful*
306 East 61st Street
New York, NY 10021
www.amyperlinantiques.com

Cove Landing—*the most wonderfully edited collection of English furniture in town*
995 Lexington Avenue (between 71st and 72nd streets)
New York, NY 10021

Madeleine Weinrib—*fun rugs, textiles and accessories*
Madeline Weinrib Atelier
ABC Carpet & Home
888 Broadway (at 19th Street)
6th Floor
New York, NY 10003
www.madelineweinrib.com

Carolina Irving—*exotic chic hand-printed linens and cottons—also the coolest embroidered and ikat tops and coats (Irving and Fine)*
John Rosselli & Associates
979 Third Avenue (between 58th and 59th streets)
Suite 1800
New York, NY 10022
www.carolinairvingtextiles.com

Claremont—*for exquisite fabrics*
1059 Third Avenue (between 62nd and 63rd streets)
2nd Floor
New York, NY 10021
www.claremontfurnishing.com

Bennison—*great old-school hand printed linens*
The Fine Arts Building
232 East 59th Street
New York, NY 10022
www.bennisonfabrics.com

Rogers and Goffigon—*the best in woven textiles as well as my go-to source for linen velvets*
979 Third Avenue (between 58th and 59th streets)
Suite 1718
New York, NY 10022

Blanche Field—*for the best handmade lampshades*
155 East 56th Street
New York, NY 10022
www.blanchefield.com

John Derian—*cool decoupage and gifts*
6 East 2nd Street
New York, NY 10003
www.johnderian.com

Nina Griscom—*very chic shop of home accessories*
958 Lexington Avenue (between 69th and 70th streets)
New York, NY 10021
www.ninagriscom.com

Moss—*a definite go-to for current and up-to-date decorative items as well as some new things you never knew you couldn't live without*
150 Greene Street
New York, NY 10012
www.mossonline.com

Amaranth—*one of my favorite restaurants on the Upper East Side*
21 East 62nd Street
New York, NY 10021
www.amaranthrestaurant.com

Sette Mezzo—*my New York kitchen!*
969 Lexington Avenue (at 70th Street)
New York, NY 10021

Sant Ambroeus—*wonderful Milanese tea sandwiches and pastries*
1000 Madison Avenue (at 77th Street)
New York, NY 10075
www.santambroeus.com

Payard—*delicious French pastries and hors'd oeuvres*
1032 Lexington Avenue (between 73rd and 74th streets)
New York, NY 10021
www.payard.com

Lupa—*my downtown Roman restaurant*
170 Thompson Street
New York, NY 10012
www.luparestaurant.com

Bergdorf Goodman—*best salads (men's department)*
Men's Store, Third Floor
754 Fifth Avenue (at 58th Street)
New York, NY 10019
www.bergdorfgoodman.com

The Wrightsman Galleries at the Met—*what more can one say?*
The Metropolitan Museum of Art
1000 Fifth Avenue (at 82nd Street)
New York, NY 10028
www.metmuseum.org

The Frick—*a place where I go to be inspired*
1 East 70th Street
New York, NY 10021
www.frick.org

ACKNOWLEDGMENTS

There was no question in my mind who I would dedicate this book to...the only issue was in which order I would list all those people who equally made everything you see possible. This work is not the result of my effort only—I am the spark, the lighting of a flame that is made of so many other elements.

Here goes...

Thank you to Doug Turshen, who had the vision years ago and encouraged me to make that dream a reality and whose guidance, talent and impeccable style brought the words, images and concepts together brilliantly—YOU made this happen.

To Leslie Stoker and Dervla Kelly, who patiently directed me through what seemed like a most daunting task, somehow managing to make it feel and appear effortless.

To Christine Pittel, who was able to help me put into words all these thoughts and articulate my visuals so appropriately and eloquently. Without her creative genius, this book would not have the distinctive voice with which it speaks.

To David Huang, who was able to punctuate the spirit of the book with unexpected juxtapositions of graphic design and endless imagination.

To my clients, without whose support and trust I could never do any of it. Many of you do project after project over the years and become such great friends and family.

To all those tremendous trades that make every piece come together, building those dreams quite literally and so beautifully.

To all the workrooms who make each and every stitch and seam and shape come to life with so much love and effort.

To all the dealers of art and furniture—antique and new—who by their passion for beautiful works help "punctuate" interiors with style and cachet.

To all the manufacturers and showrooms who so patiently assist us in every way they can to deliver on our promises and exceed expectations.

To all my staff who have made the vision into reality, and most importantly Whitney Pamula, who for over seventeen years has tirelessly supported me and whose grace, poise, and presence of mind helps us all—staff AND clients—weather the storms.

To the photographers—particularly Thibault Jeanson, who captures the passion, warmth, and spirit of my work over and over again.

To my mother, Anna Chiara Branca, the "original" spark—whose energy and support is a lifeline every day to all of us!

Last but far from least to my husband, Steve, my children and my close friends who support everything I do and encourage me every inch of the way...when I am down, they pull me up; and when I am up, they share in my joy.

PHOTOGRAPHY CREDITS

Photography by Thibault Jeanson, except:
Alan Shorthall: Pages 6, 46-47, 48, 49, 90-91, 92, 93, 188, 189, 190, 191
Grey Crawford: Pages 104, 105
John Bessler: Pages 106, 176, 177, 178-179, 180, 181, 217, 238, 240-241, 244
Melanie Acevedo: Pages 142, 143
Gordon Beall: Pages 157, 158, 159

Published in 2009 by Stewart, Tabori & Chang
An imprint of ABRAMS

All rights reserved. No portion of this book may
be reproduced, stored in a retrieval system, or
transmitted in any form or by any means, mechanical,
electronic, photocopying, recording, or otherwise,
without written permission from the publisher.

Library of Congress Cataloging-in-Publication Data

Branca, Alessandra.
New classic interiors / Alessandra Branca.
p. cm.
ISBN 978-1-58479-787-6
1. Branca, Alessandra—Themes, motives.
2. Interior decoration—Themes, motives. I. Title.
NK2004.3.B72A4 2009
747—dc22
2009014201

Text copyright © 2009 by Alessandra Branca
Photographs copyright © 2009 by Thibault Jeanson

Editor: Dervla Kelly
Designers: Doug Turshen with David Huang
Production Manager: Tina Cameron

The text of this book was composed in Bodoni,
Didot, Franklin Gothic, Interstate, Kuenstler Script,
Rockwell, and Stymie.

Printed and bound in China
10 9 8 7 6 5 4 3 2

ABRAMS
THE ART OF BOOKS SINCE 1949
115 West 18th Street
New York, NY 10011
www.abramsbooks.com